GAGG, J.
Canaller's
b
£

D1587264

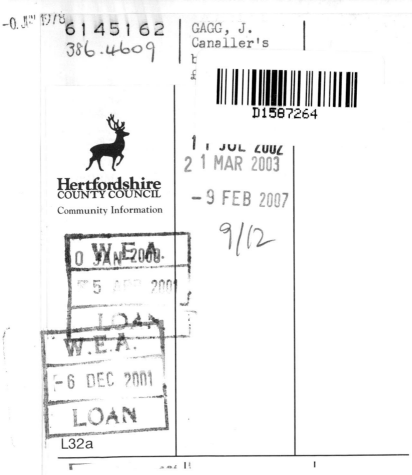

Hertfordshire
COUNTY COUNCIL
Community Information

1 1 JUL 2002
2 1 MAR 2003
-9 FEB 2007
9/12

0 JAN 2000
5 APR 2001
LOAN
W.E.A.
-6 DEC 2001
LOAN

L32a

Please renew/return this item by the last date shown.

So that your telephone call is charged at local rate, please call the numbers as set out below:

	From Area codes 01923 or 0208:	From the rest of Herts:
Renewals:	01923 471373	01438 737373
Enquiries:	01923 471333	01438 737333
Minicom:	01923 471599	01438 737599

L32b

L 33

THE
CANALLERS'
BEDSIDE BOOK

THE CANALLERS' BEDSIDE BOOK

JOHN GAGG

with line drawings by Robert Wilson
and photographs by the author

DAVID & CHARLES: NEWTON ABBOT

Also by John Gagg

Canals in Camera—1
Canals in Camera—2
5000 Miles, 3000 Locks

(for children)
Rivers in Britain
Boats and Boating
Boats and Ships

0 7153 6280 1

Set in 12/13 Bembo
and printed in Great Britain
by Ebenezer Baylis & Son Limited
The Trinity Press Worcester and London
for David & Charles (Holdings) Ltd
South Devon House Newton Abbot Devon

This book is dedicated to all those
who enjoy canals as well as being
enthusiastic about them

PREFACE

The only real fault I've ever noticed about canal addicts is a tendency to appear rather intense about it all: we talk grimly about the Nuneaton shallows and the BNC junk, about broken paddle-gear and threatened canal arms; or we solemnly discuss the exact shape of Joshers, the origins of the GUCC, or the fate of the Charnwood Forest line of the Leicester. Outsiders might be forgiven for wondering whether we actually *enjoy* our interest in canals.

Well, of course we do, but I don't see why we shouldn't look and act as if we did. Surely most of us are as interested in the gongoozlers at bridges, the angry swans at nests, the butcher's shops of Wigan and the blackberries at Tollerton as we are in restoring the Basingstoke or preserving commercial narrow boats.

This book, then, is a light-hearted pot-pourri for anyone with both a sense of humour and an interest in canals. It looks both at the Anderton lift and at polythene bags round propellers, at the Foxton staircases and at Chinese take-away meals, at the Middle Level Drains and dangling fenders, at Tom Puddings and black puddings, at paddle-gear and pubs.

I had to arrange all these things somehow, so I've put them alphabetically. There's no need to start at the beginning, then; in fact this is essentially a book for dipping into, and I hope for enjoying. Robert Wilson's drawings will, I believe, make the dips even more enjoyable.

JOHN GAGG

ANDERTON LIFT

Luckily this first alphabetical canal titbit is in fact a unique item. You find it where the Trent and Mersey Canal runs startlingly along the hillside above the River Weaver, with striking views down for miles; and it's the only boat-lift in Britain.

From early canal days the river trustees wanted a connection with the canal to avoid losing too much trade. First there was a road link to Broken Cross, where the pub of that name now sits by the canal. Later there were trucks down the hillside at Anderton, where the river is immediately below. Eventually, in 1875, a huge lift was completed, and after electrification in 1908 is still usable today. It is a 'must' for canallers, even at £3.30 return, for at least this fee helps to keep it going.

A short arm takes you into one of the tanks, each of which can hold a pair of narrow boats and 250 tons of water. Then with gates closed you start a slow 50 ft 4 in descent on the end of cables hanging from a warren of wheels, with the odd gobbet of grease dropping on you. Below, the Weaver waits, with perhaps a coaster turning by the gruesome factory opposite. When you reach the river, the gates at the other end of your tank rise to let you out, dripping a farewell down your neck as you go.

The Anderton lift takes you to another world of wide deep waters and towering ships. But up to Winsford, especially, the Weaver is worth the detour.

ANGLERS

This is a tricky subject. Basically boaters and anglers are incompatible, since boaters need waterways uncluttered by hazards,

and anglers need waterways undisturbed by boats. Yet, curiously, both need each other. For one thing, we must all combine our strength in the constant battle to keep canals alive, by using them, agitating about them, and supplying money for them. And for another, canals without boats would soon become weed-filled unfishable ditches.

So anglers and boaters live, for the most part, in friendly animosity. Boaters—we hope—try to slow down and keep as far away from floats as the shallow sides will allow (though many anglers seem to think that boats can cruise in a couple of inches of water along the far bank). And anglers—again, we hope—leave boats a little cruising space in the middle, and keep away from locks where crews have to stop, jump off, tie up, and generally go into action.

But come to think of it, this last isn't always true. Anglers seem fascinated by locks, even sitting on the mooring bollards there and making landing impossible. So it is at locks where the animosity may break out, and I've seen shaking fists at Bingley, tangled lines at Hatton, and boat-crews leaping unintentionally into tins of maggots at Audlem.

I'm sorry that I only see it as a boater. Perhaps we ought to change places regularly. Then my angling friends would know what it is like to come suddenly on a rod sticking out of a vast screen of reeds or willowherb, with no sign of the human at the other end. It's especially alarming if he's asleep and thus loses his line to our prop. Those ghostly hands that emerge equally unexpectedly from the 6 ft growth, flinging loaves of bread around —they too make our hair stand on end. With the unmown towpaths nowadays we can't always see you, that's the trouble.

Where the towpath is clear, however, what can be pleasanter than to come on a fishing competition, with anglers every few yards for miles, rigid and alert, green-umbrella-ed and oilskinned, surrounded by keep-nets, baskets, wrappings and polythene bags? Unless, of course, you have to get your hired boat back to its base that evening.

ANGLESEY BASIN

If you ever decide to swing round the northern outposts of the Birmingham Canal Navigations you will not only find a fascinating cruising area but a surprising number of cows and fields. There are, however, factories, vast rubbish tips, old workings and high-rise flats as well, and under a pile of these flats is Catshill Junction in the road-riddled town of Brownhills. You are on the Wyrley & Essington Canal here, and you can take it eastwards for a mile before it gives up the ghost at the top of the old Ogley Locks. This is a pity, for you could once have descended them and joined the Coventry Canal to Fradley. But there is compensation, for you must turn left instead to the Anglesey Branch.

This $1\frac{1}{2}$-mile waterway was once a feeder from the reservoir, but Lord Anglesey wanted to move his coal, so it was made navigable in 1850. Coal went on moving most of the time till 1967, and as you cruise up the branch, you can see the remains of chutes where it was brought by lorry in later years. Beware also the remains of boats, but look out for a lively and independent canal carrier who may well be loading still, to sell by the hundredweight along the canals as he travels.

The water is clear, and cookers and television sets can be seen under you as you pass a housing estate on your approach to the basin at the end. But the terminus is lonely and spectacular, with the dam of what is now the sports complex of Chasewater rising high above you. The water bubbles into the fine broad basin, choppy with waves in a wind. You can moor peacefully here, with waste land all round, probably full of history.

AQUEDUCTS

Canals, like earlier roads and later railways, often came to streams and rivers and had to cross over them. Sometimes they found themselves crossing over roads, and later a few railways burrowed under them. All this meant that bridges had to be built to hold the water, and there are far more of these about than we realise.

Most of them traverse small streams, and are usually unnoticed from a cruiser. Others take the water over quite wide rivers and even valleys, and some have become famous attractions to motorists as well as canallers. Two of them—Pontcysyllte and the Barton Swing Aqueduct—have places of their own in this book, but there are several others that are quite striking, especially from the ground level below the canal.

Edstone (or Bearley), on the National Trust route to Stratford, is a miniature Pontcysyllte, travelling over two railways and a road in an iron trough on stone pillars (see the plate). It also has, rather startlingly, a towpath below water level, so that a crew member can walk alongside your boat with his head at the waterline. Another iron trough, short and sharp, takes the Grand Union over the Great Ouse near Wolverton, in place of nine locks which once were there; and a magnificent arched masonry aqueduct, 600 ft long, carries the Lancaster Canal over the River Lune.

There's a solid aqueduct for the Coventry across the River Tame near Tamworth, a little one next to a lock at Yarningale on the Stratford, two over the River Aire at different places for the Leeds & Liverpool, one for the Grand Union over the Avon near Warwick (with perhaps connecting locks one day?), a tricky one on a bend over the Trent near Rugeley—and dozens of others, striking or insignificant, along the canal system.

Usually you're able to spot the bigger ones because of the narrowing of the channel, and often you can only just slide a 7-ft beam boat through. But Brindley was more generous when he crossed the Dove near Burton-on-Trent, and many a traveller there fails to notice the river passing under nine fine arches.

I've never counted all the aqueducts, but there must be hundreds.

ARMITAGE TUNNEL

This is just a note by way of a requiem. Until 1972 there was a charming little tunnel at Armitage near Rugeley on the Trent & Mersey. It was only 130 yd long, but it was thought to be the earliest tunnel on our canals; it wriggled its way in uneven rock through a little hill crossed at an angle by a main road.

Over the years, however, the pounding of heavier and heavier lorries wasn't doing it any good, and girders were put in a few years ago to try and keep it usable. Unhappily, this didn't seem to work, and now, forlorn and sad, its top has gone except where a new and horrid concrete bridge carries the road.

At its former entrance the *Plum Pudding* still serves beer and simple meals, and across the road the well-known *Farmhouse Restaurant* offers food of wide renown. But of the Armitage only tall reproachful dark-red rock walls survive. What happened to the bats that used to live inside it, nobody knows.

BALANCE BEAMS

One of the greatest delights of working through locks is to lie flat on a broad warm balance beam, waiting for the waters to level. You can do this on several canals, such as the Grand Union and the Leeds & Liverpool, but you have to be rather thin to manage it at some of the narrow canal locks. The most frustrating beams for this purpose, however, must be the telegraph poles

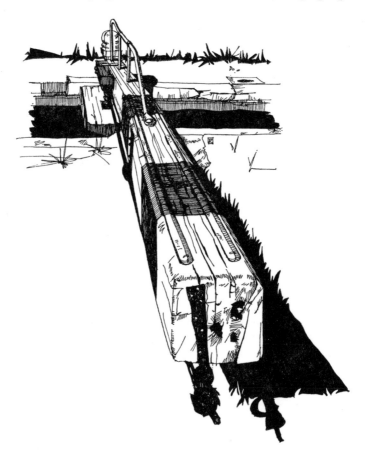

used on the Kennet & Avon, the Upper Avon, and the Exeter Ship Canal. The ugly metal beams which often replace old wooden ones now are not only too narrow but also too cold and comfortless to lie on.

These balancing arms of lock gates are an interesting study as you change from one canal to another, or even as you move along a single canal. The finest are huge square-sectioned masses of oak, but there are many other varieties. Those on the Leeds & Liverpool and the BCN seem to lie down at lower angles than most, and running up the BCN from West Bromwich to Walsall the arms seem much longer than usual in proportion to the gates. Tardebigge arms bend sideways at a slight angle, while down the Staffs & Worcs—and indeed at many other odd spots—you come across quite stubby sawn-off ones, which have been shortened to allow for road widenings.

It is more usual when a bridge has been widened, however, to make a right-angled bend in the beam, which then looks extremely odd. You'll see this at Kinver, Gailey (ugly metal ones, these), and Stratford-upon-Avon; but at Blackburn and elsewhere the beams have been entirely removed to widen the road, in favour of a curved cogged rack to be wound with your windlass.

Concrete is another unnatural latecomer to balance beams; it is either packed in metal beams to make up the weight, or even pushed into rotting holes in wooden ones. But whatever the make or shape of a beam, moving it is still a very satisfying job. If you're lucky, you have a row of ridges on the ground to push your feet against, though more likely you'll have a trench worn by generations of other feet. The backside is the best part of the body to push with, and there's no point in heaving and struggling, for you'll never get a beam to move faster than it wants to.

Just shuffle along gently, like the man on the colossal 13-ft beams at Crinan lock in Scotland.

BARGES

Nothing annoys a canal boater more than to be asked by a

naïve friend whether he goes cruising on 'a barge'. Yet for some reason every non-canaller, and every newspaper reporter, calls every canal boat a barge.

For the record—though I don't know that there's a law about it—a barge on a canal is normally 14 ft wide, and therefore highly unlikely to be found among the 7-ft locks throughout most of our canal system.

What all our non-canalling friends and reporters are referring to when they talk about barges are usually the 70-ft by 7-ft boats, which they ought to call 'narrow boats' (see p 96), 'monkey boats' or 'longboats'. I don't suppose it really matters, though, but it's just one of those things, like asking the proud owner of a new car how he likes driving his lorry.

BARTON SWING AQUEDUCT

Pontcysyllte aqueduct is deservedly spoken of with some awe, but Barton in industrial Lancashire is also worth a glance. The original aqueduct here was opened in 1761 to carry the Bridge-water Canal over the Mersey & Irwell Navigation, and men thought it almost an engineering miracle. It left room for the flats to sail underneath through a 63-ft-wide arch, and people were apparently astonished that no water dripped from the canal above. 'Vessels o'er vessels, water under water' amazed everyone.

They would have been even more amazed in 1893, for by then the vast Manchester Ship Canal had taken the place of the Mersey & Irwell Navigation; and, as the ancient aqueduct would have carved off the masts of seagoing vessels approaching Manchester, it had to go. After debating the possibility of a high crossing with lifts at each end, it was eventually decided to cross on the existing level, but to make a section of the canal to swing open like any road swing bridge.

Thus, in its new form, the aqueduct remains still a remarkable sight. Unlike the Anderton Lift with its rising gates, the water at each end of Barton is sealed off by two swinging gates rather like lock gates, worked electrically. When both seals are made, the

ANDERTON LIFT

AQUEDUCT   (EDSTONE)

BARGES

BARTON SWING AQUEDUCT

whole huge tank, 1,450 tons and 235 ft long, pivots open, while waiting Bridgewater canal boats watch vessels pass through on the Ship Canal. Then, if you're lucky, there's time to swing it closed, open the gates, and sail across.

The actual crossing is rather an anti-climax, as the girders all round you cut off any strong impression of what lies beneath. I'm sorry to say, too, that you won't be allowed to have your boat in the tank for a swinging ride. So the crossing of Barton, anyway, compares badly with that of Pontcysyllte, where on one side there appears to be nothing beneath you at all.

The bridge-keeper, I believe, is also responsible for the nearby road swing bridge, and sometimes takes a bit of finding. Another snag about Barton is that it closes for a week or two in the middle of summer for its annual overhaul, to coincide with local holidays. This must be awkward for happy-go-lucky cruisers expecting all waterways to be open.

BASINS

Basins are places where the waterway widens, either at a terminus or as a sort of layby on the route. Once, of course, they were busy loading areas surrounded by warehouses, but now their fate varies. At towns such as Banbury and Oxford they are filled in and covered with tarmac, buses and buildings. At an equally sad number of places—especially in the Black Country— they are choked with reeds, bricks, oil-drums, tyres, prams and old cars. Luckily—as at Market Harborough, Shardlow, Braunston, Aylesbury, Retford, Nantwich, Lincoln, Gloucester and Stourport (but why not Whaley Bridge?)—many still contain boats.

Some basins are neat and tidy moorings, supervised and served by an efficient boatyard. Others look like a free-for-all, with new and derelict boats tied up higgledy-piggledy, and the debris of long-gone boaters making slipways and quays hazardous or even inaccessible. For some reason, wherever two or three boaters are gathered together without a firm supervisory hand, they produce what looks like a junk yard. Maybe that's why some

2

local authorities are still convinced that the canals are entirely inhabited by undesirable characters.

BEARDS

One of the interesting aspects of a canal cruise is that it provides a man with a suitable opportunity to grow a beard. When he is at work, the inevitable early sproutings arouse ribald comment, but in the anonymity and seclusion of a boat on the canals these crucial days can be painlessly passed. Thus you will often see an unshaven face at the tiller of a passing boat, or peering more coyly from a window, on its way to achieving a beard.

A less pleasing development sometimes occurs when men find themselves steering a traditional narrow boat conversion for the first time, and get carried away. Imagining themselves to be 'real' boatmen, they not only grow beards but also cease to wash, and take to wearing ragged and dirty clothes. This not only gives the canals a bad reputation, but must cause many of the neat and tidy old boatmen to turn in their graves.

BIG LOCK

If you travel through Harecastle and down the twinned locks of Heartbreak Hill, you come in time to Middlewich (not to be confused with Nantwich on the Shropshire Union or Northwich on the River Weaver). Here, in addition to yet another pub called the *Cheshire Cheese*, there is a curious lock $\frac{1}{2}$-mile beyond the town centre. Unlike the previous sixty-eight since Stenson it is a broad lock, and, therefore, called Big Lock. But why? Can or could broad-beam barges from further north ever use it? Seeking the answer to this is an intriguing cruising task.

Travelling further you come to Croxton Aqueduct, which is too narrow to pass boats much wider than 7-ft. This narrowing is of recent origin, however, so once upon a time the 14-footers could pass. You go on, therefore, to the Anderton Lift, and here you find the tanks are wide enough to bring 14-ft-beam boats up from the Weaver. So it seems that from the Weaver, at least, when Croxton Aqueduct was wider, broad boats could come and pass Big Lock to Middlewich centre, though of course no further.

The rest of the Trent & Mersey is a mystery, however. It was dug as a 'broad' canal, linking with the Bridgewater and even with plans to cross the Mersey. But in fact the three tunnels of Barnton, Saltersford and Preston Brook are neither one thing nor the other. They will certainly not pass 14-ft boats, as two cruising 7-footers rashly trying to go opposite ways still occasionally find. And it appears that in the days of their building there were complaints that boatbuilders had made their boats too wide for the tunnels—9-ft beam is the accepted limit for them now.

So poor 'Big Lock' stands unused by big boats; 14-footers could never, in any case, have come from the Bridgewater, and, once Croxton was narrowed, they couldn't even come from the Weaver up the Anderton Lift. But Big Lock is an interesting lock to come across, with a pub of the same name alongside, and an awkward bottom gate which has its own special opening device of a chain on a drum turned by a handle.

BINGLEY FIVE-RISE

Most of us are used to the sudden appearances of gongoozlers (see p 66) after miles of emptiness—especially at locks and at weekends. Bingley Five-rise is one of these gongoozler-spots, and at almost any time in the year you can be sure of an audience as you puzzle out how to get your boat through these remarkable locks.

They are in the form of a staircase (see p 122)—the largest broad-lock staircase south of the Scottish border. Enormous cliff-like gates separate each lock from the one above it, and descending weirs at the side help to remove any surplus water. Footbridges across each lock serve as grandstands for the watchers, who thus effectively block the passage of crew members rushing madly from one side to the other. What with capstan-type worm-and-cog ground-cloughs at the sides, and those huge scissor-like sideways-sliding cloughs in the gates, not to mention the possibility of putting water in the wrong place, the crew usually has to be pretty nippy.

There are complicated diagrams and instructions in the handbooks on how to work this formidable staircase, but I've never yet met anybody who really understood them. Most people seem to cope, however, and the job in the end seems to be less harassing than at, say, Grindley Brook or Bratch. Unlike the narrow canal staircases you can actually amuse yourself by passing another boat going in the opposite direction, if your boats are both narrow-beam ones—which is quite an experience in a lock.

Bingley is one of the Wonders of the Waterways, but I have two rather less important memories of it. Once an angler at the foot of the locks took such umbrage at the appearance of a boat that he shook his fist and wished all boats at the bottom of the cut; and on another occasion—if I didn't dream it—I actually met a caravan, complete with wheels, sailing up to Bingley firmly fixed to the hull of a traditional 14-ft-beam Leeds & Liverpool short boat.

BIRDS

Plenty of ordinary birds fly about the canals, perhaps, like us, taking refuge from more harassing areas; but some of the birds we see are particularly addicted to water. Of these, moorhens (or water hens) are the commonest, wagging away with their tails and abandoning their fluffy chicks as a boat approaches. In spring you'll see their nests, often precariously built on odd reeds or submerged tangles of branches; a bird will swim purposefully across in front of you with some specially selected nest ingredient held in its beak. Then come the eggs and the swimming balls of fluff, which grow up into large brown birds looking entirely different from their parents before they at last change into the same clothes.

Coots, with their white beaks, are not so common, though you'll see quite a few in the reservoir by the Grand Union above Calcutt locks. Another fairly rare bird is the heron, but sometimes you'll see one standing by the water and peering intently in. It

will take off and fly lazily away ahead of you, only to land and stand again. It does this so often that you're not quite sure whether it's the same heron or a new one.

The swans are the birds with character—and sometimes pretty tough characters at that. They build themselves great mounds of nests and sit on their huge eggs at the very edge of the canal; sometimes one of them will guard his domain fiercely. A notorious swan on the Leicester used to flap furiously after boats, and even peck nastily at them. Another was well known on the Chesterfield as Herbert the Dreadful and Belligerent Swan.

Most swans seem harmless, however, and will hang around for scraps, but it's as well to keep away from their formidable beaks. A swan taking off is almost as remarkable a sight as a jumbo jet, and its use of its feet as brakes when landing is equally intriguing. The cygnets are lovably ugly furry creatures before they grow their feathers, and they—like the moorhens—remain a different colour from the adults for a long time.

Ducks and colourful drakes potter about, take off and land, and you'll certainly see wagtails wagging away by the waterside, and swallows zooming and diving for insects right down to water level. But you'll be lucky if you see a grebe. Indeed, if you do, he'll vanish smartly under the water, and you'll twist your neck trying to see where he comes up again.

BIRMINGHAM CANAL NAVIGATIONS

The curiously lonely, varied maze of the BCN needs a book to itself, and here I can only dip and whet the appetite. But if you can put up with the occasional propeller-tangle of wire or polythene, the mysterious underwater jolt, oil in the canal in places and a few sordid views, you will be rewarded by perhaps the most intriguing cruising in the country.

You are in the Black Country, but not of it. You can moor in the heart of Birmingham in near silence. You can cruise for miles without seeing a soul from the roaring mass of traffic and factories that any road journey through the area reveals. You scratch your head and refuse to believe that you are in Britain's industrial heart.

But you are. The reason for the quietness is that the canals which made the Black Country have now been abandoned by their factories, so that areas of peaceful emptiness now border them in places. Motorways have stolen some of this land, but even they are inaudible on their concrete stilts. Gorse and bracken hide the rubble, and access from the canals to the shops is sometimes a problem.

From the fine development by the *Longboat* near Broad Street in Birmingham, the Main Line strides almost straight to Wolverhampton, to drop down twenty-one locks to the Staffs & Worcs. All round this Main Line there are permutations and combinations leading off to northern outposts such as Anglesey and Pelsall, and through exits in all directions, with the southern ones piercing hills by Dudley and Netherton Tunnels. There are odd tail-ends such as Titford Pool, Engine Branch, Bumblehole and Coombeswood, as well as ways out to Stourport, Worcester, Stratford, London, Nottingham and Manchester, showing how this was and is the centre of the canal system.

There are oddments of the BCN elsewhere in this book. It may well be that there are enthusiasts who never leave the area, for it certainly grows on you.

BLACK DELPH

From time to time every canaller probably decides on his favourite canal spot—though this may change regularly. The Audlem flight was once high on my list, until I met it on a Sunday for a change. Sharpness Old Basin, too, is a stimulating place, where you feel you've come to the very end of the whole waterway system as you sit high above the wild Severn estuary; and Bumblehole, looking across at the no-man's-land around, can be a wonderful spot on a crisp sunny morning. But the eight locks at Black Delph not far away have been for a time at the top of my list.

This pile of locks—which used to be nine until 1858, when they were turned into eight, though local people still call them 'The Nine'—is at the end of the BCN, where the Dudley No 1 Canal comes down past the vanished Two Lock line, through Round Oak steelworks, and then into the equally fascinating Stourbridge Canal.

There's a mooring at the top of Black Delph where you can overlook a great dip full of trees, though a few yards either way you're back into industry. Then you have to crawl under a widened main road bridge to work the top lock. When you emerge from this, you see a vast panorama stretching southwards away to hills that seem to have no connection with the Black Country. This southerly view from the top lock is spectacular enough, and the view back up the locks from the bridge at the bottom is also unforgettable.

If you are travelling upwards, and someone is lock-wheeling for you, every time he empties a lock you get a great foaming torrent over the broad weir at the side of the lock below him. At other times the trickle of water over these weirs weaves its way over long tresses of weed, which also have a curious beauty. So the view up these eight deep locks stacked one on top of the other can be quite startling, with locks on the right of the pile separated by high steep steps from the little niagaras on the left. The whole out-of-this-world scene is set off by towering blocks of flats to one side, from which I swear I once heard somebody cry 'Help! Murder!'

I was rather less enchanted by Black Delph on my last journey: some foul polluter had filled the waterway above with a mass of oil, which was slowly covering the steep lock-walls all down the flight, and the bottom lock was surrounded by the kind of nuisance-making gongoozlers that the canals can well do without. But if you've never tried Black Delph locks, have a look at them. Even the name makes your toes tingle.

BLISWORTH TUNNEL

Until Dudley Tunnel came back into action, Blisworth on the Grand Union remained for a long time the longest tunnel in normal use. It is 3,056 yd long and takes about half an hour to negotiate, unless you happen to be following a pair of loaded narrow boats with a faulty engine, as I once did. On that occasion my journey took $1\frac{1}{2}$ hours amid clouds of diesel fumes.

At intervals there are ventilation shafts, which on the ground above can be seen as chimneys. In the tunnel beneath they are often waterfalls, and an umbrella is helpful for the steerer. At intervals, too, there are great metal plates counting off the yards by hundreds.

When you enter Blisworth, you may often find it impossible to see the other end for some time, unless it is a bright day and no other boat has been through for a while. On misty and/or fume-filled days it is even impossible to see either end from the middle.

The digging of this tunnel held up the completion of the canal for 5 years, while boats had to be unloaded and the goods taken over the hill on a plate railway for reloading into other boats at the opposite end. There is no towpath, but narrow boats can pass each other in the tunnel. In pre-motor days, of course, leggers waited at the ends for business to arrive.

BOLLARDS

Solid metal rope-grooved mushrooms at Wigan, frail gnarled wooden pillars on the Coventry, engraved neat quiet posts on the Stratford, great coaster-holding monsters on the Sharpness, sad new utility concrete ones everywhere—these are the bollards up and down the country, though rarely where you want to moor for the night.

The metal ones of the Leeds & Liverpool—like so many things on that solid canal—look as if they will last for ever, as do those at the locks on the Nene. Wooden bollards still remaining, however, totter to extinction, and even the new concrete ones are frequently uprooted by over-eager boats. Current policy seems to provide bollards outside locks only, for tying up while the lock is prepared. Oddly these are often ignored, so that some new bollards on Hatton soon vanished in the nettles and brambles. More useful, especially at broad locks, would be more bollards on the lock sides; but often there are none, and those that exist are wrongly placed to hold most pleasure cruisers from charging the gates.

The smooth new bollards at the broad-lock end of the Trent & Mersey serve at least as handy seats for anglers, as anyone trying to get into Stenson Lock will testify.

BOOKS

If you are a fanatic, your collection will have grown steadily in recent years, as author after author has discovered what has been there all along. But even if you are only a moderate enthusiast, there's a certain basic library that no reasonable canaller should be without.

Heading the list should be that classic which really brought today's new canal mania into being—L. T. C. Rolt's *Narrow Boat*, with its remarkable account (for those days) of cruising on inland waterways; and alongside Rolt—though not for light reading—will be the massive *Inland Waterways of Great Britain*, by L. A. Edwards. This, recently brought up to date, contains every imaginable fact and statistic (except for the depths of locks) about every inch of navigable inland waterway in the country, and about quite a few unnavigable ones, too. It quotes you the Manchester Ship Canal Act 1960, the distance from Gwastad Lock No 30 to Crindau Bridge on the derelict Monmouthshire Canal, the constitution of the Thames Conservancy, and all about the sixteen named branches of the Witham Navigable Drains. It takes every waterway in turn and tells you all you want to know about it, from its origins to its present state, from its tunnels to its speed limit, and ends up with a distance table showing the landmarks every few furlongs from one end to the other. 'Edwards', more than any other single book, might be called the statistical bible of the inland waterways.

If Edwards has written the statistical bible, Hadfield is undoubtedly the Recording Angel. There must be a whole row of Charles Hadfield's books on any canaller's shelf, from the general *British Canals* through the complete range of regional histories, giving the most fascinating details of the beginnings and subsequent development of our astonishing canal network.

You can dip blindly anywhere in Charles Hadfield's works and come up with intriguing gems, from Fowler's experiment with a cable on the bed of the Bridgewater to the one-time purchase of the upper Avon for £5,000 by seven men, including the vicar of Wootten Wawen; from the attempts to carry coal waggons on rafts on the Somersetshire Coal Canal to the fact that the Leeds & Liverpool now runs for over 10 miles on what was originally part of the Lancaster Canal. You can read of defaulting shareholders, absconding treasurers, fighting boatmen, underpaid lockkeepers and dismissed engineers. You can, in vivid imagination, dig the Standedge Tunnel (and take a slice off it and then add a longer slice later), try all kinds of lifts and slopes to avoid building locks, and stay awake at nights sorting out the incredible maze of the BCN. The whole vast tangled web of the rise and decline of our canals is all there, somewhere or other, in Hadfield.

There are three other books that could be thought of as pictorial appendices to Hadfield—*Canal and River Craft in Pictures* by Hugh McKnight, *Canals and their Architecture* by Robert Harris, and the almost-a-classic, *The Canals of England* by Eric de Maré. As a sad end-piece to a history shelf, Ronald Russell's *Lost Canals of England and Wales* reminds us of all the waterways we might still be cruising on if we had ever had any politicians with European imagination.

If your interest lies only in canals as they are today, and in journeying on them, you doubtless have Frederic Doerflinger's *Slow Boat Through England* and *Slow Boat Through Pennine Waters*, which both leave you breathless with their wealth of cruising facts. John Liley's *Journeys of the Swan* is a boisterous account of rougher travels on a well known unconverted narrow boat, while David Owen's *Water Highways* and *Water Rallies*, John Seymour's *Voyage into England*, and John Hankinson's *Canal Cruising*, not to mention John Gagg's *5,000 Miles, 3,000 Locks*, take you up and down this canal and that, and past a great variety of present-day locks and junctions, tunnels and pubs, boatyards and anglers, swans, villages and towns. Perhaps, if I dare go so far, my own two *Canals in Camera* books may act as suitable bookends to the section dealing with cruising on canals today.

Finally, of course, your guidebooks. Rather sadly, British Waterways phased out their useful booklets on individual canals, and replaced them with *Guides to the Waterways* in four parts. These may be improvements in a number of ways if you have good eyesight or a magnifying glass, don't mind reading a map upwards while you read about it downwards, and are very fond of pubs. But fortunately Ladyline have jumped into the breach and brought out separate booklets on the popular canals; these are extremely readable and easy to use, as well as being very helpful in their details. Perhaps the most useful potted guide, however, is *The Canals Book*, which comes out afresh each year— brought up to date—and which contains an amazing amount of information, in map and text, on the whole waterway system apart from the Thames and Broads, which have separate books.

My basic bookshelf has grown over-long, and I still see many more out of the corner of my eye that I might be tempted to name. But I'll be content with adding one remarkable publication, which unfortunately doesn't fit on any kind of bookshelf. This is *Waterways Heritage*, by Peter Smith, published by the Luton Museum and Art Gallery, and indeed printed at the Town Hall, Luton—an astonishing production measuring 20 in by 11 in, with 82 pages, and containing an interesting pot-pourri of mainly historical canal material. You must see it for yourself; besides being fascinated you'll no doubt be left wondering, like me, why it was published in Luton and not, say, in Birmingham, Manchester, Coventry, Stoke-on-Trent, Stourport, Oxford or even Rugeley—somewhere with a canal, anyway.

BRAUNSTON

This is a hallowed name in canal circles, both ancient and modern. A village in the middle of nowhere, first touched by the Oxford Canal, it was in 1793 authorised as the starting point of the mighty Grand Junction route to London, now part of the Grand Union. So all through the canal era it saw much traffic, and must have been one of the busiest water junctions in the country.

Today it is equally busy and well known, though its traffic comprises pleasure cruisers, few of which fail to pass by there at some time or other. The well known *Rose and Castle* has extended its canal trade by adding that incredible restaurant on the canal bank. Around the flight of locks much narrow-boat activity still goes on, but now for holiday use. Braunston's chief modern claim to fame lies in one man—Michael Streat—for it was at this village that he produced, in a former dock and reservoirs, one of the very pleasing pioneering pleasure cruiser bases before the boom really started.

Michael's name will undoubtedly go down in canal history, and many of us remember with admiration and even affection the Blue Line complex, which hummed with activity when such undertakings were precarious in the extreme. He laid out safe and pleasant moorings, provided good hire cruisers, offered reliable and inexpensive service, and even kept pairs of narrow boats trading in the days when almost every other 'boatyard' was little more than a nervous length of towpath.

Many thousands of canal enthusiasts joined the canals through Michael's work, and it may well be that we are not appreciative enough of the enormous influence he must have had, directly and indirectly, on the life of the canals today.

'Blue Line' and 'Braunston' were synonymous, seemingly indelible parts of the canal scene. But there came a time when the famous firm amalgamated with a lively newcomer, Ladyline, and many canallers were disconcerted to see that the name 'Blue Line' was discarded. This was an unfortunate bit of psychology, but business presumably had its reasons.

So 'Blue Line' vanished, as did the well known pairs of commercial boats and a number of familiar faces. Braunston will never be the same again, though many will remember it.

BRATCH

When you've done Bingley and Foxton, you will think you've seen everything in the way of lock staircases. Well, probably you have, except for the Caledonian. But what do you make of the group of three locks on the Staffs & Worcs known as 'The Bratch'? They are neither staircase nor ordinary locks, for, although they have pounds between them, these are much too short for anything but a bathtub. So you must have the next lock's gates open before you can leave the one before. Don't anticipate

this, though, when coming downhill, for the top gate of the lower lock can block the culvert which takes the upper lock water into a long side pond out of the way. If you do block this culvert and the lower lock is full, then the water from the upper lock is going to pour all over the countryside.

There's another snag about the Bratch. As with other narrow-lock staircases, some boaters don't realise that once a boat has started through the flight nobody else can come in at the other end. Because of the steepness of the slope, and the intervening bridges, it is also impossible for anyone at the top to see anyone at the bottom, and vice versa. So a stream of boats can easily play follow-my-leader into one end while purple-faced steerers at the other end can wait all day.

There has to be a lot of give-and-take at the Bratch, then, and I often wonder how many bloody fights used to occur among boatmen—or how many do now? The striking octagonal toll house at the top must have seen, and continue to see, many an amusing sight.

BRIDGE NAMES

The most useful clues to your whereabouts on the canals are the little numberplates on the bridges, but not all canals have these. The Bridgewater has no identification on its bridges, nor has the Chesterfield, so you are permanently worried as to where you are.

The Birmingham Canal Navigations go in for magnificent number-plaques on their buildings, but content themselves with small nameplates on bridges—and not many of these are left. You can spot them here and there, however; they reach out along the Birmingham & Fazeley Canal into the heart of the country. Indeed, a few rusting plates—Dixons, Balls, Dunstall and others—still cling to the bridges the B & F provided when they built $5\frac{1}{2}$ miles of the Coventry's route from Fazeley to Whittington Brook.

The finest bridge names are undoubtedly on the Staffs & Worcs Canal. Massive oval plates, with numbers also, label Giggetty, Bumblehole, Wombourne, Botterham, Dimmingsdale, and many other of the hundred-odd, fascinatingly named bridges of this remarkably varied canal. Painted often in black and gold, long may they be preserved.

BRIDGE NOTICES

On the Llangollen near Wrenbury there's a notice by a lift bridge which states: 'This bridge is insufficient to carry a traction engine or any other extraordinary weight'. This is perhaps the oddest notice I remember, at least for modern eyes, but bridges everywhere offer an interesting harvest of notices. The trouble is, of course, that you rarely see them unless you go ashore.

The commonest, still, are almost certainly those quaint diamond-shaped notices issued under some Motor Car Acts at the turn of the century. A fascinating mixture of formidable capitals and rows of tiny letters, they are marvellously confusing with their various tonnages and axle weights, and one imagines many a driver stopping and puzzling out whether he dare place his axles or wheels on the bridge or not.

The Shroppie, however (a rich source of notices of many kinds), doesn't bother about such precise instructions, on many bridges merely telling you that your weight must not exceed that of 'the ordinary traffic of the district'. Since every district nowadays seems to contain 30-ton lorries, it's perhaps as well that nobody reads the notices—at least from a vehicle.

Yet another Llangollen notice—very decrepit the last time I saw it—must take the prize for simplicity and clarity: 'Boatmen

BLACK DELPH

BUMBLEHOLE   (BCN)

COWS

FACTORY   (MARPLE)

must put this lift up bridge down carefully after their boat has passed under'. Now what could be clearer than that? And wouldn't it be a good idea to repeat it all down the Oxford lift bridges, and even (amended) at every lock gate and paddle-rack?

Bridges are among the few places on canals where the new impinges on the old, so modern notices have begun to appear. There are those tall lollipop erections, for example, which try to keep heavy lorries from the old humpbacked bridges by stating axle-weight limits in the new European gobbledy-gook red rings, and bar track-laying vehicles in plain English. Then there are those well meant but utterly ignored new notices at lift bridges and swing bridges, pointing out that only authorised persons are allowed to operate them. These have had little effect on small boys, who swing them and drop them just for the hell of it whenever they have a spare moment.

BRIDGE NUMBERS

When you travel along roads, you are overwhelmed by identification signs. The signs aren't so generous with distances nowadays, but entrances to villages and towns are labelled, and signposts at junctions and crossroads help you to pinpoint almost to the yard your exact place on the map.

It's much more complicated along canals. They don't often run through villages or towns for a start, many mileposts have

3

long since disappeared, and junctions are rare, let alone crossroads. So most of the time you are between one point and another, and nowhere exactly.

Hire firms fail to point this out clearly enough to beginners, and many a time I have been asked by puzzled steerers, 'Where are we?' The only solution to this problem—apart from highly skilled map-reading with 1-in Ordnance maps—lies in identifying the bridges. Luckily, most of these still show their invaluable numbers, and these are the chief locating devices on the canal system. You need your *Canals Book* or *Guide to the Waterways*, of course, where the bridge numbers are given; and then, provided some hooligan hasn't removed the number from the next bridge, you can quickly check up where you are.

These numbers, like much else, manage to vary somewhat from canal to canal. The Leeds & Liverpool numbers are bold but rather confusing, since many of them are followed by letters of the alphabet (I have never been able to discover why, except that the bridges with letters seem to have been later additions in various towns). There are ancient carved numbers on some canals, and I remember one bridge on the Trent & Mersey where the carved number disagreed with the more modern one.

On the northern Oxford the numbers jump upwards rather rapidly, since many are missing in the meandering stretches of canal that were straightened at one time. There are plain painted numbers on the Worcester & Birmingham (though you'd do better to go by the lock numbers so helpfully strewn along Tardebigge). Most of the standard little oval plates of British Waterways still have solid raised metal figures, like the old railway and canal notices in the days when things were made solidly and well, instead of pathetically perishable.

I hope canal maintenance will continue to include these numbers, or the cut may be strewn with lost boaters sadly looking for home.

BUMBLEHOLE

There are in fact two Bumbleholes known to me on the canals.

One of them is a 10-ft-deep lock (and nearby bridge) below Bratch locks and on the way to Giggetty Bridge on that canal of so many strange names, the Staffs & Worcs. The other is an oddly isolated place in the southern realms of the BCN, now occupied by a small boatyard run by an interesting canal enthusiast.

This latter Bumblehole used to be part of the main line of the Dudley No 2 Canal as it went off to join the Worcester & Birmingham at Selly Oak, but when Netherton Tunnel was built, the canal was straightened and left Bumblehole as a loop. Part of this sank later, leaving a little bit near Windmill End now curiously called the Boshboil Arm, and a $\frac{1}{4}$-mile hook at the other which now leads you, under the lowest bridge for many miles, through tall reeds to the boatyard.

If you creep up there, you'll find an ancient crane, a replica of a BCN toll house, perhaps a beautifully built and decorated narrow boat or two, and, if you need it, helpful service. You can look out towards Cobb's Engine House over the mouth of Netherton Tunnel, and across high grass-grown dumps from the many pits that used to fill the area. There's even a farm on a distant hill and a golf course climbing up it. The Black Country might be miles away, though if you search around you'll find a road outside, with traffic. If you stick to the canal, however, there's no need to touch civilisation at all.

The name Bumblehole must have an origin, but I confess I've not yet discovered it.

BUTTY see NARROW BOATS

CHINESE RESTAURANTS

The high mandarin in Hong Kong or wherever who supplies the tons of identical foods to the thousands of Chinese restaurants in Britain may know nothing of canalling. But since he invented 'hot-take-away' Chinese food, he has had the blessing of many a boater. It's surprising how often, within a few minutes of the towpath, there are chop suey and fried rice, king prawns and noodles, on tap, all in their hot cardboard-topped foil dishes, ready to travel in their little carrier bags back to your boat. So with no gas and hardly any washing up you can still set a large hot meal in front of you.

At Birstall and Stourport, Newark and Worcester, Gloucester and Aylesbury, and at almost every calling place much bigger than a village, there's a Great Wall, a Hong Kong or a Golden House, lurking behind its curtains and inscrutably offering its 100-item menu. It's all a lot dearer than it used to be, and somehow you feel hungry again after the next five locks, but it's a change from fish and chips. At Burton-on-Trent, however, a Chinese restaurant sells these, too.

CLOUGHS see GATE-PADDLES and GROUND PADDLES

COGS AND CATCHES

Most paddles at locks lift upwards, and their own weight would drop them down again if some form of catch wasn't provided to hold them up. The provision of such a catch seems to have stirred the ingenuity of canal engineers. On parts of the Shropshire Union there is merely a bit of metal hanging on a chain, to be jammed in the cogs of the mechanism. But, for contrast, in the north of the same canal there are savage-looking hooks to swing over and hold the cogs.

The most common device on gate-paddles is a small pawl resting on a cog of its own towards the end of the spindle. If this is placed on before winding, the paddle doesn't crash down even if your windlass slips—as it may often do on worn Trent & Mersey spindles. The Oxford gate-paddles have two unusual devices, one in the form of a sliding spanner and the other a square hole which hinges over to grip a small square spindle of its own.

Some pawls are designed so that they come into place automatically as you wind up the paddle, but most have to be placed in position. With a pawl in place, the paddle-rack rises with a satisfying musical clatter, but if a worn one slips, the paddle descends with an unsatisfying cacophonous crash.

Well greased paddle-gear may (or may not) work well, but

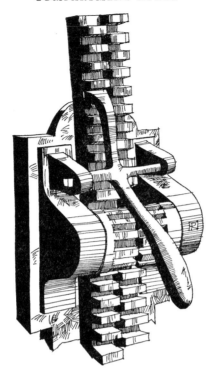

the grease soon transfers itself to your fingers as you connect or disconnect the variety of catches on your journey. Those who wish to preserve their hands are advised to wear gloves.

COMPARTMENT BOATS

Even those who know little about canals are likely to have heard about 'Tom Puddings', though few will have heard of William Bartholomew, their inventor. Yet he, more than anyone, built up the prosperity of the Aire & Calder Navigation when other canals were falling by the wayside.

He was a remarkable man, much neglected by history, and even by the canal and the port of Goole, where he created so much. Sadly, even the Tom Puddings themselves are in decline, as North Sea Gas begins to reduce the demand for the coal that these curious little boats carried for so long.

From 1865 the strange trains of square metal boxes began to run from collieries on the waterway to ingenious unloaders at Goole, which lifted them out of the water bodily and tipped their coal into colliers. They ran to such effect that 1,000 of them were carrying $1\frac{1}{2}$ million tons of coal just before World War I, and they virtually made Goole into the port that it is today.

Amazingly, no one seems to know why they were called Tom Puddings, unless they were thought to look like basins. They look as unlike boats as it is possible to look, but a long string of them, preceded by dummy bows and a tug, could carry an enormous quantity of coal when loaded down to the last inch. They snaked along the waterway and packed themselves into locks, discharging their coal at Goole with great speed. But increasingly nowadays you'll see them sadly lined up in long rows here and there, looking forlorn and unwanted.

Even before the demand for coal began to drop at Goole, brassy newcomers had started to challenge the century-long reign of the Tom Puddings. These were much larger containers, fastened rigidly together in a line of three, and pushed by what is oddly called a 'pusher-tug'—though how a 'tug' can 'push' I can't quite see. This new form of compartment boat can be seen unloading coal at Ferrybridge with a modern version of the old Goole hoist, and similar 100-ton units are now pushed down to the Humber with various loads. There they can be lifted bodily on board ships, and taken over to Continental canals and rivers.

The Tom Puddings themselves may be fading away, but they did not live in vain. It may even be that the large new containers will develop a massive trade from the Yorkshire canals and the Trent to the Continent—a trade that would certainly gladden W. H. Bartholomew's heart.

COWS

An odd canal subject, perhaps, but there are few canal cruises free from these animals. Usually you see them standing knee-deep in the water, obviously having brought in a great deal of the adjoining field over the years—though they seem wise enough not to step out into the deeper channel in the middle. If you happen to moor to the field which they inhabit, you discover that they are the most inquisitive animals imaginable, especially if they're young. In no time they are snuffling at your window and trampling all over your ropes and mooring pins, and they'll happily do this for hours. They stand there contemplating you as you take well deserved refreshment at the end of the day. Sometimes they chew a little as they stand, and often they drool gently on your side deck or down your windowpanes. If you try to drive them away, they reluctantly move off a yard or two before returning immediately.

The largest population of inquisitive cows is down the River Nene, where it seems almost impossible to moor without attracting them. If you don't like cows on the canals, of course, you can always tie up on the towpath side. But I've even seen them there. They're quite harmless, unless one happens to be a bull, but in the many places where they have had access to locksides they make lock-working a rather messy activity, and we once found one down Tardebigge that had actually fallen in a lock.

There is a famous historical canal cow, which every book concerned with canals is in duty bound to mention. This one, in 1912, fell into the cut at one end of Foulridge tunnel on the Leeds & Liverpool, and managed to swim through to the other end. There it was revived with a good strong drink, and the incident is now recorded in the local pub.

DRAWBRIDGES see MOVING BRIDGES

DREDGERS

Now and again—though unhappily rarely—you meet a dredger, trying to tackle an Augean task which really needs fifty more of its brothers. The usual type seems to have legs that let down to the bed of the canal while it dives a sort of predatory beak under water to remove some of the silt. This is sometimes placed on the bank where it either forms rich land for a farmer or a high towpath for the canaller (as on the Trent & Mersey near Weston).

Or it is put into hoppers to be taken off by a tug to a distant grab, which scoops it up for the second time to deposit it in its final resting place.

This dredger-cum-hopper-cum-tug-cum-grab operation is presumably unavoidable in places, but it always seems to me to be one of the most time-consuming operations imaginable. Every helping of silt has to be handled twice, as well as being laboriously

moved for some distance along the waterway. Work out for yourself the time and labour involved in this, and multiply the answer by the vast quantity of silt still waiting patiently to be taken out of our canals all over the country.

Come to think of it, the silt has all come in from the canal banks; so why can't it just be put back there again? But wherever it goes, a few more dredgers wouldn't come amiss, or we shall all be taking to canoes.

I suppose we have in fact come quite a long way from the days

FLASH   (TRENT AND MERSEY)

FLYOVER   (BCN)

FOOTBRIDGE

FOXTON

HARECASTLE

HIRE BOATS

ICE

JUNCTION   (NORTON)

when dredging was done with a sort of large spoon suspended from a boat. I've seen great dredgers scooping away in the Trent, a sucking monster on the Gloucester-Sharpness, and occasional draglines from the bank here and there. It's just that we need more of all of them.

EAGRE

Most people seem to spell this *aegre* or *aegir*, but the dictionaries and encyclopedias stick to *eagre*, so I've done the same. Whichever way it's spelt, it isn't in fact a canal item, though it's very much the concern of canallers. When you come to visit the Chesterfield, the eastern end of the Leeds & Liverpool, or the canals of the north-east, you need to mug up on the eagre, which is the Trent's answer to the Severn Bore.

Roughly speaking it's the tide from the sea rolling up the Trent on top of the river trying to roll down. It shows up only at high tides (over 26 ft measured at Hull), but it can be quite dangerous to canal boats downstream of Gainsborough then. Anyone who is rash enough to come across an eagre by accident should face it head-on—that is, with bows down river—and be prepared for a buffeting if not worse. It is especially dangerous to be moored at that time.

Eagres are essentially phenomena to be admired from land—at Owston Ferry, for example—as they roll up in great waves, breaking at the sides. In any case, if you are on a boat going down Trent from the final lock at Cromwell, you'd be rash to set out without taking advice. Even on the majority of days when there is no eagre there's still a tide running up and back again, and you'd be wasting your energy and fuel battling against it.

So anyone for points north should chat with the helpful lock-keeper at Cromwell, and set out so as to use the ebb to get down the river. Similarly, the obvious thing is to leave Keadby or West Stockwith locks when coming up river at just the right time to ride with the incoming flood. The keepers at these two locks will tell you the best times to leave.

You'll probably come across some bright chap who couldn't

be bothered. He'll be aground, maybe, or out of fuel. And he may be even worse off if he happens to bump into an eagre.

ENGINES

Unless you're young and fit or own a horse, you probably use an engine of some kind to move your boat along. This is an interesting field of study.

There are several canal vessels around driven by steam, for, like railways, the waterways attract all kinds of nostalgic experimenters. If you keep your eyes skinned, you'll also find craft pushed along by paddle-wheels, or water-jets, or by those ancient diesel engines that have to be started by blowlamps.

Most of us unimaginative chaps, however, rely on common-or-garden modern engines driving propellers. But even here we have quite a variety. There are engines driven by petrol, engines driven by diesel oil, engines driven by mixtures of petrol and oil, and engines driven by paraffin. Some live in large engine-rooms of their own on converted narrow boats, or under the sink or in the lavatory in the interior of less spacious craft. Others manage to sit nearer the stern and out of the way by being connected to a Z-drive propeller-leg instead of to the traditional long shaft. Still others can be brought from home tucked under your arm and hooked on the boat when you feel like it—engine, propeller and all.

These last belong to the famous—if not notorious—category of 'outboards'. They're extremely handy, can't be stolen if you've taken them away, and have a thirst for fuel that convinces you they were invented by petrol companies. On canals in particular this can be infuriating at times, as you stagger across the fields to Fleckney on the Leicester, or stand dangerously on your roof on the Shroppie, hopefully looking for a distant Esso sign. It pays to carry three or four 5-gallon tanks and fill them up at every chance. In my outboard days I learnt the way across many a muddy field and rural footpath, so that my charts are dotted with symbols reminding me where garages lurk.

Inboard petrol engines are not so greedy, but they worry

many people by their potential danger if fuel leaks anywhere and hangs around in the bilges unable to escape. So diesel oil is my favourite fuel now, and I think favoured by many others.

A diesel engine costs more to start with, but it seems to run for ever without a refill. Indeed, you tend to forget to look at your gauge; a diesel engine running out of fuel involves all kinds of mysterious jobs known as 'bleeding', but so far—touch wood—I haven't managed to run out of fuel, and since it's about half price anyway if it's put tax-free straight into your tank, you feel that running your engine is almost as cheap as using a horse, with the price of hay what it is.

The fuel is liable to throw out soot from the exhaust, I haven't the faintest idea how diesel engines work (they do it without sparks, it seems), but they seem to chug away happily all day long and I've certainly never experienced any of the alleged smell which anti-diesel boaters talk about. I put a few gallons in the tank now and again and leave the rest to the engine.

FACTORIES

Once upon a time anyone proposing to start up a factory would be most likely to build it by a canal, or at least to have his own canal branch. Networks like the BCN flourished on the service they gave to factories. Now, ironically, a factory alongside a canal is a comparatively rare sight. No doubt all the original ones have fallen down, and even if they have been replaced or rebuilt, they now turn their backs on the water.

In built-up areas, therefore, there are still occasional stretches of gaunt buildings rearing straight up from the canal's edge. Jones & Shufflebottom's stretch along the towpath in Stoke-on-Trent, and Gardners' Sausage Machines accompany the beginning of the Old Main Line at Tipton—or so large notices say. But some of the names still visible on massive factory walls are now so faded that the presence of any activity behind the wall is doubtful.

Not all these factories present blank walls to the boater. There are often broken windows or other openings, from which startled faces appear. They're a friendly lot, these gnomes along the cut, dressed in various mysterious uniforms and carrying variegated tools of their unknown trade. Behind them in the depths odd machines clunk and clatter, and pipes and conveyor belts wander about. At sunny lunch times the gnomes emerge and sit among the grit and oil and rubbish lining the canal, for all the world as if it was Brighton beach—and they turn out to be perfectly ordinary people.

Occasionally there are no masking walls, and a cruise through Bilston steelworks in full blast is a remarkable experience. Even weirder are some of the gurgling mazes of pipes on the Trent & Mersey near Northwich, and on the Shropshire Union entering Ellesmere Port; while the range of smells on the Staffs & Worcs near Calf Heath is work enough for your nose as you negotiate a tar distillery in the heart of the country.

My favourite factory is at Armitage, where quite unexpectedly you pass under several storeys of glass windows stacked high with ceramic wares. Baths, wash-basins and lavatories all stand there in row after row, upside down and presumably waiting for lorries to take them out into the transport rat-race of the roads. What an interesting contrast you can meet in Stoke-on-Trent, where Johnson's still carry fragile china by water between two of their factories on the Caldon, loaded on a fascinating catamaran called *Milton Maid*. Maybe, when the roads grind at last to a standstill, other factories will turn again to safer and cheaper water transport.

FARMER'S BRIDGE

Most people breathe this name with awe after its long exposure on television and in articles in the national, boating and architectural press. Canal enthusiasts, unfortunately, seem to regard it as a symbol of a great new restoration of canals from one end of the country to the other.

Let's look at it, however. Farmer's Bridge is a junction in the heart of Birmingham where a considerable amount of canalside tidying-up and building has taken place, including huge blocks of flats, a canal-oriented pub, and a pleasant sitting-out and walking area. Virtually nothing, as far as I can discover, has been done to the navigation channel.

Well, this is very wonderful, and at least it shows that a local authority has begun to take notice of the canal banks, even if it isn't able to do much between those banks. Moreover, lots of other local authorities have been able to cast their eyes on Farmer's Bridge, and many are beginning to realise that their canals can be part of an exciting scene.

Good, good—and thanks to Birmingham for this bright example. But there's one important next step for all local authorities that have suddenly discovered their canals. They must remind themselves that canals are places for boats to move along, and not just bits of water to build flats and plant bushes alongside. Canals need boats, and unless Farmer's-Bridge-type schemes everywhere include long distances of the navigation channel in their plans, those boats are going to have a struggle to get to them.

Some local authorities, such as Stoke-on-Trent, are putting money into canal restoration as well as towpath titivation. Unless everyone begins to act in the same way, we shall end up with a lot of fancy parks around shallow isolated duckponds.

Keep taking boats to Farmer's Bridge, then, as well as buses; and walk round the corner through the tunnel under Broad Street to see a more canal-like atmosphere at Gas Street Basin, where narrow boats actually live, and where Worcester Bar once kept alive the bitter rivalries of canal companies. For here, where you can sail through now, boats once had to unload over a physical bar in the waterway.

FENDERS

I was always taught that it simply wasn't done to cruise along with rows of fenders dangling, and that all the best crews immediately took up all fenders and coiled all ropes as soon as the boat got under way. Thus I still feel a slight grating of the teeth when I see the very common sight of a cruiser moving with half-a-dozen white sausages hanging down on either side.

The captain may have good reason for this, of course. He may have decided that his fenders are better hanging down than lying on the narrow side-deck for people to trip over. Or more likely he may feel that his boat is such a bad shape for canals (as many are) that he prefers to use dangling fenders as perpetual protection for his hull—even at the risk of jamming in locks.

True canal boats certainly had no fenders, except at bow and stern for ramming lock gates. They relied on their sturdy and properly shaped hulls for sliding into locks and through bridge-holes. It's a pity that so many modern cruisers are thoughtlessly based on seagoing shapes instead of on the slab-sided shape of a narrow boat. But even those that are the right shape for canals and canal locks are often not tough enough to stand up to the wear and tear on their hulls.

This is where two or three well placed rubbing-strakes can be well worth their cost—even though cunningly protruding bolts on lock gates always manage to get in between them. Strakes along the hull sides, with extra lengths at the stern corners and at the upward curve of the bows, will take most of the clouts that bridges, locks and quaysides can offer, though they need to be capped with metal to prevent them from being worn away entirely.

With such rubbing-strakes you don't really need any fenders, except a couple for occasional use at night to prevent the gentle grinding of your strake on concrete from keeping you awake. I must say, though, that despite my early training I travel with a fender hanging near the front at each side to protect the curve under the bows. This is where I come in to drop crews at locks, or merely to moor, and if you look at canal boats, you'll notice that most of them are much more savagely scarred here than anywhere else. Oddly, few boatbuilders apart from Dawncraft seem to bother about protecting this vulnerable spot. So my dangling front fenders have saved me many a gouge.

The other vulnerable spots—the extreme back corners—seem almost beyond protection. Those fat bulges you can buy to fix there are only too easily dragged off, and anyhow you really need them all the way up each corner. So canallers are resigned to a constant erosion here as they scrape on the many hazards at bridges and locks, at various heights. The only slight safeguard is to watch the steering a bit more. Or, of course, you can always buy a couple of dozen old motor tyres and fix them in a continuous belt all round.

FIELD BRIDGES

Away from main roads the most likely clue to the existence of a canal is a humpbacked bridge. Some carry normal country roads and have recently needed weight-restricting notices; but most are used only by cows, sheep and tractors.

These bridges are among the most attractive landmarks of most canals, and although the basic brick design may be repeated hundreds of times, there are still the occasional individualists, such as the slightly sagging bridge near the Heyfords, the brick-pillared one at Awebridge, Whittington Horse Bridge, the bridge with barely the archway left (if that now?) near Marston Doles, and others with variations of railings, wire-netting, or more pleasant brick patterns instead of the normal brick parapet.

On the Stratford, of course, simple cantilevered metal bridges are fairly common, with no towpath, but a slit for the towrope. The Trent and Mersey too, goes in for utility bridges with no towpath, but with no slit either.

There's room for a small book on canal bridges—especially these rural ones with their sudden tractors, their drooling cows or their surprised courting couples. If they were all swept away, canal cruising would be considerably less friendly and interesting.

FLASHES

This is, I believe, a northern term (though found on the Basingstoke also), oddly appropriate for stretches of water where the ground has sunk, especially in salt-mining areas. You can see such lakes around you from the Trent & Mersey as it approaches the Weaver, though in two or three places subsidences have actually taken place by the canal, causing the waterway to bulge out sideways. Near Marston, in fact, a new length of canal had to be cut in 1958, since the other channel was disappearing into a collapsing shaft.

There are two large flashes at the upper end of the Weaver, and you can glimpse one of them down below you from the Middlewich branch canal. Better, you can cruise up the Weaver into the lower flash, though the sides are very shallow. Small boats can sometimes reach the upper flash if they can find the channel.

The flashes on the Trent & Mersey are deceptive. You may feel you can cruise away from the towpath into the tempting little lake, but don't try it. One at least seems to be filled with rubbish, and another is a gruesome graveyard of narrow boats, with some of their skeletons still showing above water.

FLOWERS

Even in the driest summers the banks of canals grow huge luscious plants getting on for 6 ft high. Anyone with the slightest interest in nature study will take along a flower identification book, and will have a profitable cruise. Most of us, too, probably take large vases for the flags and meadowsweet that grow in profusion along the way.

Almost everything grows near the canal, from policeman's helmet above Stourport to huge primroses in the Shroppie cuttings, with wild garlic mixing with the chemical smells approaching Pontcysyllte. Of course, the flowers that specialise in waterways are the most common and the most striking. The

aforementioned yellow flags appeal to me more than their duller iris sisters in our gardens, and forget-me-nots look much happier along the towpath than tamed in our spring beds.

The cleaner canals often rival rivers in places, with their waterlilies bobbing respectfully in our wash, and even the reeds and rushes have their own various little flowers if you search among the great blades of their leaves. It seems impossible, though, to do anything for the poor old bulrush, whose name continues to be taken in vain by almost everybody.

4

The real bulrush, or *scirpus lacustris*, has in fact a fairly insignificant head of little flowers, and that dark brown sausage on a stalk, which everyone calls a bulrush, isn't a bulrush at all but the flower of the reed-mace. You'll find it in Wormleighton reservoir and not far from Crick tunnel, among many other places; but I'm afraid people will still go on calling it a bulrush.

FLYOVERS

When they started to build flyover bridges on motorways, we thought they were ingenious ideas. Yet a much more complicated flyover was completed on the Birmingham Canal in 1829, and you can travel on it to this day.

The old line from Birmingham to Wolverhampton had meandered about like a drunken sailor, partly round the contours and partly to serve as many places as possible. Its climb up six locks at Smethwick and down six locks again led to endless delays and quarrels, however, so by 1790 this level had been lowered in two stages, leaving only a climb of three locks. This was thought to be an incredible piece of earth-moving, but between 1827 and 1829 an even vaster job was completed.

This feat of engineering consisted of a huge cutting for the canal past Smethwick, a wide towpath each side, a remarkable bridge over the lot, and finally an even more remarkable passage for this new waterway underneath the old one where it curved round on its way to Oldbury. So the old line of the canal became a flyover to the new one on the Stewart aqueduct; and by an ironic coincidence a motorway (see p 90) now flies even higher over both canals.

There are two other canal flyovers that work in the same way. One is up the Caldon Canal where the Leek branch leaves at the head of the three Hazelhurst locks and then crosses over the main line, which is by then lower down. Curiously this lower level, as with the Stewart, was dug at a later stage, when the main line's course was changed and taken under the embankment already carrying the Leek branch.

The other flyover takes a branch from the Trent & Mersey to

the official start of the Macclesfield near Kidsgrove. Its crossing of the main line of the T & M is mysterious. As you come from Harecastle towards the Macclesfield, you would expect to fork right, but in fact you turn left at right-angles just before the first downhill lock. You then curve round, and eventually, after the T & M has dropped through three locks, you cross it on the Red Bull aqueduct, reaching the Macclesfield proper at the 1-ft stop-lock at Hall Green. There must have been some reason why you couldn't just have forked right instead, but I've yet to discover it.

FOG

Nobody is likely to smash into you from behind with 30 tons of sheet steel, or overtake you in the fast lane doing 90 mph, but fog on the canals has its lesser problems. If you're steering a longish boat from the stern, indeed, you can barely see your bows, let alone anything in front of them. Some canals wind about so sharply that following their bends can be a harassing business; and, of course, meeting another boat in the narrow channel is an alarming possibility. Nor is working a lock in a fog much fun—though doing it by yourself and in the dark is even less amusing.

On the whole, then, it's as well to moor and read a good book if thick fog descends. You may, however, be on your way from the Stainforth & Keadby to the Chesterfield or further up the Trent. If so, you must lock out of Keadby to catch the tide, fog or no fog. The Trent may be wider than canals, but a foggy journey up it can still be a strain, since heavy barges also travel there.

They are likely to be coming up from behind, using the same tide, which is better than their approaching you from the opposite direction. They are obviously not the same menace as the lorries on foggy motorways, but they certainly keep you looking apprehensively over your shoulder. Moreover, riding up a foggy river can also mean that you can't see either bank at times, and if you move over to find one, you may go aground if the water is still low.

The marvellous compensation for an unexpected fog on the canals—and this can happen even in August—is the view when it begins to lift. If the sun is coming through at the same time, the sight of the fog, whirling and wisping away from the waterway in front of you, is memorable. You are still isolated in its cocoon as it slowly retreats, and it seems to fend off the whole horrible supermarkety, juggernauty, rat-racing world.

FOOTBRIDGES

There are all kinds of bridges for vehicles along the canal system, but those for people are almost as intriguing. Occasionally, like Bridge 105 near Lower Shuckburgh on the Grand Union, they are for non-canalling pedestrians to get from one side to the other, but more often they're at locks for the use of canal crews.

The crudest type is a couple of pieces of wood fastened to the lock gates, and without any kind of handrail, as near Fradley on the Trent & Mersey. This forces you to do a quick tightrope walk across. The Leeds & Liverpool, however, doesn't hold out risks like this, but provides great solid crossings clear of the bottom gates, with formidable rails to hold on to, as the drawing shows. Bosley flight on the Macclesfield has a fine metal bridge, without a handrail but wide enough to give you confidence; and Chester has some even better bridges with good railings.

The Trent & Mersey in Heartbreak Hill and elsewhere has separate broad footbridges, but these are wooden with a slit in the middle for towropes if the two halves haven't sunk together. Foxton and Watford flights have solid footbridges with solid side-rails, causing much rude language from those who normally tow their boats in and out with ropes. Split footbridges tend to lose their gaps after a time, and some of the delightful slim ones on the Staffs & Worcs seem to be sadly fading away. There are still a few of these cantilevered metal footbridges about, however, even though they have often been crudely repaired.

Two interesting variations of the 'rope-slit' idea can be seen in the Tardebigge flight and at Tipton Factory locks. The former is wooden, the latter has curved low side-rails. In each case the bridge is cantilevered the full width of the lock shoulder, leaving room at the far end for the rope to be slipped under.

Although there is a wide variety of these independent footbridges, the great majority of locks in fact rely on the bridge fixed to the gates—though few are as precarious as the rail-less T & M one mentioned already. The northern Staffs & Worcs and Tardebigge gate-crossings are very solid blocks of wood, but on some parts of the T & M and the Oxford the planks look more precarious, and you're glad to have a handrail to hang on to.

One of the infuriating things about the otherwise admirable Leeds & Liverpool is that it gives you a sturdy way of crossing the lock tail clear of the gates, but then often provides you with nothing at all at the other end, whereas at most locks you can cross somehow at both ends. So as you slog your way up Wigan you either walk miles round the bottoms of the locks, or balance precariously along the very top of the top lock gates.

One problem of footbridges fixed to the gates is that they open when the gate does. This offers dangerous opportunities of leaping from the opened half of the plank to the half that is still closed, to save going round the far end of the lock. This is possible if you have long legs and a head for heights, and especially if you wisely reach out with a hand to catch the handrail at the same time, but the possible consequences of missing your footing or slipping on wet wood are slightly alarming.

Where there are gate-paddles as well as a gate footbridge, the layout is interesting. Some ingenious engineers arrange things so that you inevitably remove most of the paddle-grease as you pass by, especially if you are wearing a bulky windbreaker or rainwear. The alternative is to lean out like a racing yachtsman when passing the cogs and racks.

FOULRIDGE see COWS

FOXTON

Even those canallers who hate history are bound to admit that there are certain places, such as Harecastle, Anderton, Barton and Stourport, which grip even the dullest imagination. Foxton is another of them.

Today you meet it as an exciting and invigorating—and perhaps at times infuriating—experience, after a long and largely featureless level pound from the top of the Watford flight. Undoubtedly, despite the possible crowds of gongoozlers, there's something both eerie and memorable about this collection of locks sliding so rapidly down a steep hillside.

There must be a lot of ghostly chaps arguing around these locks, for Foxton was at the centre of many plans and counterplans. The broad waterways from the Trent to Market Harborough were always supposed to have gone on and joined the southern canals somehow or other, but they ended up by being linked through narrow locks only from Foxton to Norton Junction on the present Grand Union. People very soon regretted those narrow locks, and talked often of widening them.

Instead, eventually, they decided to build an inclined plane at Foxton to carry barges if necessary, and to do something about the Watford locks later. After a large working model of it was tried out at Bulbourne, the Foxton inclined plane was built, to be opened in 1900.

It must have been thought an incredible device at the time, carrying boats in tanks up or down a 307-ft slope that raised or lowered them 75 ft 2 in. This was supposed to be done inside

12 minutes, which must have been a great improvement on the time taken to traverse ten locks, but unhappily the company never widened the Watford locks, the traffic didn't grow sufficiently, the cost of keeping up steam was high, and by 1910 the plane had virtually ceased to be used and the locks were in action again. The bits and pieces were in the end sold off for £250.

Now you can go and search for the foundations among the bushes and trees and find very little, though some clearance has been done. The ten locks we now use would be Britain's record staircase but for the invaluable passing-place in the middle that makes it two staircases of five instead, providing endless entertainment for spectators all summer. By an ingenious arrangement you don't have to take lockfuls of water all the way down as in other staircases, but, instead, each lock has an elongated sort of reservoir at the side which stores water or releases it to save wastage all the way down the flight.

If you follow the instructions and work smartly, it's surprising how quickly you can pass through these locks. Like Harecastle tunnel, however, you won't pass through at all if you enter either group of five after somebody has already started at the other end. For unlike Bingley, only canoes can pass in the staircases themselves.

FUEL see ENGINES

GAS STREET see FARMER'S BRIDGE

GATE-PADDLES

Water runs in and out of locks either through holes in the gates or through channels in the ground. In both cases the openings have to be covered or uncovered to suit your needs, and the machinery provided for doing this forms one of the most intriguing studies on the waterways.

The basic aim is simple. You have to move some sort of a shutter away from some sort of a hole, and in almost every case, on gates, this is done by sliding the covering upwards. This cover is way down there on the end of a long rod, and it is the bits and pieces at the top of the rod that connect up with the person who is dealing with the lock.

These bits and pieces work in a variety of ways. Normally the top of the rod has a vertical slab of teeth called a rack, with which large or small cogs (or both) mesh so as to pull it upwards, and the shutter with it. The gearing may be high or low—thus affecting the

quality of your work—but the cogs all work from a square but tapered spindle on which you put your windlass to do the turning—unless you are using a handspike on the Calder & Hebble. This square bit may be quite close to the cogs, in which case you have to stand precariously out on the gate, as on the Southern Stratford. It may be on the end of a longer spindle, which enables you to stand on land, or on an even longer one extending to the end of the balance beam, or even lurking under it as on the Trent & Mersey.

Sometimes you get two lots of mechanism for good measure, pulling up two racks and two shutters with one lot of windlass-turning, as in places on the Grand Union. You may find two paddles to a gate on the Staffs & Worcs, but you sometimes have to wind them separately. Make sure, too, before you swing the windlass too vigorously, that there's plenty of clearance for your knuckles.

Not all gate-paddles work with this cog-and-rising-rack system. There are various experimental designs about, mysteriously enclosed, so that you can't be quite sure how they're working. Some (for example, on the Brecon & Abergavenny) are said to work by compressed air through long thin tubes. You raise the shutter at Welches Dam in the Middle level by turning a large nut at the top, and there's a flood lock on the Wey where you heave the thing up bodily, rather like the sections lifted out of weirs to control water flow.

The Leeds & Liverpool, as usual, uses an entirely different principle on most of its gates. Instead of a shutter sliding upwards there is a huge piece of wood pivoted like half a pair of scissors, and sliding sideways parallel with the lock gate until the opening is uncovered. This is done in two different ways. In one case a very long toothed rack runs horizontally alongside the balance beam, and is pulled along in simple fashion by a handle and a cog. The other end of the rack pulls the top end of the 'half-scissor', which obligingly moves over at the bottom end. The same result is obtained in other places by a curved set of teeth engaging with the handle.

The 'rising rack' gate-paddles must be kept up in some way, or they'll soon crash down again. For thoughts on this matter, see COGS AND CATCHES. When the times comes to close the openings, the paddles should be wound down again, despite the misleading word 'drop' that remains on some notices. Dropping paddles with a crash may have been common in the days of thorough maintenance, but nowadays it is only done by gnarled boatmen, if any, and a few pleasure-boaters showing off.

It is possible, however, to lower some paddles by gripping the spindle extension after lifting the catch, and letting it turn in the palms to control the descent of the rack. To do this you need either gloves or asbestos palms.

GONGOOZLERS

This is a common canal name, of obscure origin, for that sprinkling of people who appear here and there on canals just idly gazing at you. Usually they stand at bridges, and at certain places at weekends they sometimes amount to far more than a sprinkling.

The unfortunate thing is, of course, that they are attracted especially to locks. Thus on a fine Sunday in August you may find yourself trying to work through the lock into the Avon at Stratford with half America and Birmingham watching you. A few people lining a bridge are one thing, but a pushing and shoving crowd is another, especially on lock edges and round gates. You may have some difficulty swinging balance beams without knocking a few of them in. They'll trip over your ropes, too, and for heaven's sake don't put a windlass down, or it will be borrowed as a souvenir or accidentally kicked in.

When gongoozlers are in manageable numbers, their conversation is interesting. Usually one of them explains to the others exactly how the lock works, only somehow they seem to get it all wrong. You can of course pretend they're not there, or instead you can set out to put them right, and eventually enrol them as IWA members. There is always a leavening of children, of course, some of whom eagerly beg you to 'Gi's a lift, mister!' I mention these younger gongoozlers under KIDS.

The great thing about gongoozlers is that once you have the gates closed and the paddles down you can leave them behind you. Unless, that is, you happen to be in a flight of locks, when they have an endearing habit of following you all the way down.

GROUND PADDLES

Instead of making holes in the gates—or sometimes in addition to them—lock builders often made passages in the ground to move water in or out of locks. These little tunnels are mysterious places, exposed to view only if you happen to visit a lock under repair. In the tunnel somewhere, as across the holes in gates, must be a shutter to stop or release the flow of water; and as with gate-paddles these shutters are connected on the ground above to some form of operating mechanism.

Often this gear is similar to that on gate-paddles, with the exception that there is no need to have a long extension spindle to reach the operator, as most gate-paddles do. Most common, again, is the vertical rack of teeth, meshing with cogs in various gearings to drag it upwards. The square tapered spindle—

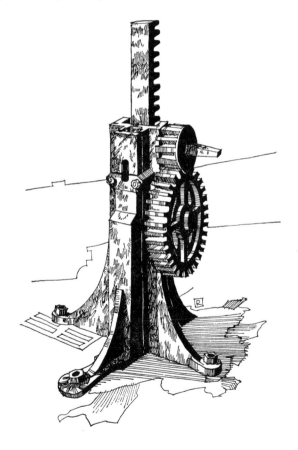

sometimes more round than square through use—is there to take your windlass, and indeed there is often a spindle on either side so that two people can actually wind up the paddle at the same time—a very welcome possibility in places.

A ground paddle variation which is hardly ever seen on gate-paddles is the use of a vertical worm gear instead of a toothed rack at the top of the rod coming out of the ground. You will find these (though you can't see them inside their protective casings) on the Warwickshire Grand Union (see HATTON, p 71), and there are more visible ones alongside many locks on the Leeds & Liverpool. The Grand Union ones are worked by turning the windlass on a spindle in the normal way, but those on the L & L are operated differently. Sometimes there is an ordinary windlass-type handle on top of them, to be turned in a horizontal plane as you lean out over the lock side, but at other locks there is a bar across the top that you twist round as if tightening or opening an old-fashioned press. In both cases you are precariously near what is often a long drop, especially when you crane over the lock to see if the thing is working or not.

This isn't the only type of ground paddle—or 'jack clough' as they say up north—offered by the Leeds & Liverpool. At the top end of many locks there is a kind of 'half-scissor' sliding board similar to that found on so many gates on this canal; but the ground paddle version is opened by heaving up a wooden arm to a vertical position, and sometimes the water pressure is so great that you need brute strength to do this.

Again, with vertical rack-type ground paddles, there have to be gadgets for stopping racks from crashing down again (see COGS AND CATCHES).

GRP

These mysterious letters, I am told, stand for glass-reinforced plastic, which most people casually (and I gather wrongly) call 'fibre-glass'. This is a modern artificial material still sneered at by many boaters, but which confounds them by increasingly ousting other boatbuilding materials.

Aesthetically it may not match the look of wood, but on the other hand it doesn't open at the seams or corners and put you on the bottom, and its ability to bounce off bridges, locks, towpaths and other boats commends it especially to canallers. A GRP hull is a one-piece jointless unit which you don't even have to paint. The only thing to watch is obtaining reputable GRP to start with, and not the kind that varies in thickness from an inch to next to nothing, giving hull-sides that seem to wave gently along their length.

GRP boat-owners are almost always happy with their hulls. But they still hear mutterings of 'noddy-boat' from others cruising by, with their bilges slopping with water and their annual painting and leak-stopping bills still in their pockets.

GUILLOTINE GATES

Rare on canals, but common on rivers in the Fens, this form of lock gate explains itself by its name. It slides up its tall framework and acts as its own paddle-gear, letting the water in or out as the gate starts to rise. The River Nene is the daddy of guillotine-locked waterways, with thirty-eight lifting gates at the bottom ends of its locks, massively raised by endless turns of a (fortunately) well-oiled handle—and equally massively lowered.

There are two famous guillotine locks on the canals. At one the gate now stays precariously open over the one-time stop-lock into the Stratford Canal at Kings Norton, seen in the drawing. The other, at Thurlwood on the Trent & Mersey, is a huge metal box with rising gates at each end, built to counteract shifting ground. A vast bolting device makes sure that you can't open both ends at once, but many nervous boaters prefer to use the ordinary lock alongside, which seems to work perfectly well.

On the Calder & Hebble is a lesser known guillotine, electrically worked and installed when a widened road sabotaged ordinary gates and beams; and at the Anderton lift the tanks are sealed off by guillotines. All these lifting gates, as you pass under them, dribble a pattern on you and your boat.

HARECASTLE

Even if people have hardly heard of anywhere else on the canals they've probably heard of Harecastle, for it has the advantage of being both historically and currently fascinating.

When the first Harecastle tunnel was built on the Trent & Mersey, it was reckoned the longest tunnel ever dug, at nearly $1\frac{3}{4}$ miles. Brindley, who started it but unhappily didn't live to see it finished, heard people wax both ecstatic and sarcastic about it. He adopted the most remarkable methods for those days, using beam, wind and water pumps to pump out great quantities of water that flooded in, and lighting fires to cause updraughts for ventilation. He even dug tunnels from the canal line to the nearby colliery.

Despite all the doubts about 'castles in the air', the tunnel was at last finished, so that the whole magnificent Trent & Mersey—

the Grand Trunk—was opened in 1777, 11 years after the tunnel had been started. It was a narrow tunnel, and because boats couldn't pass each other, it soon became a notorious bottleneck. 'Legging' a boat through took 3 hours, for which a man was paid $7\frac{1}{2}$p and probably lost a few pounds in sweat. So in 1827 a new parallel tunnel built by Telford was opened, and this in contrast took only 2 years to build.

Boats from the north were still legged through the old tunnel for a time, but those in the other direction could be towed through on the towpath that had been incorporated. The old tunnel gradually became impassable in the early part of this century, and boats through the new one all had to be pulled by an electrically driven tug, steam being considered dangerous because of the poor ventilation. The first of these tugs had to take a barge with it carrying 18 tons of batteries, but later it took its current from overhead wires. It would tow up to thirty boats at a time at $2\frac{1}{2}$p each, and it pulled itself along on a cable on the canal bed.

There is now a pumping station at the south end for ventilation, great doors being closed when it operates. The towpath has gradually been removed as it has collapsed. A notorious dip of the roof, 1,300 yd into the tunnel, is a hazard for many boats now. There is a gauge at each end for you to try for size, and also notices giving times at which boats may pass in each direction. Woe betide the boater who ignores them, for he may well have to back all the way out again.

Just to help the whole eerie business the canal water along here is almost blood-red, and there's a thundering great railway tunnel not far away whose trains can frighten the life out of you as they suddenly appear and roar over the canal at the northern end.

HATTON

This, along with others such as Tardebigge and Wigan (see pp 133 and 147) is one of those flights of locks spoken of with awe or boasts wherever boaters meet. This particular collection consists

of twenty-one Golden Steps to Heaven, which have in fact followed on the heels of another twenty-five locks if you've just come from Braunston. Hence so many boats resting at the *Cape of Good Hope* for the night at the near-halfway mark.

Hatton is distinguished firstly because the narrow locks were all rebuilt as broad locks in the 1930s in an unbelievable burst of canal optimism, and secondly because its locks have some of the most striking paddle-gear in the country. Both these facts, as it happens, make for comparatively easy lock-work, for although the Hatton paddles need a good many turns, the enclosed gear does seem to work more smoothly than some of its battered and rusty colleagues elsewhere.

The gates are heavy, of course, as you'd expect on broad locks, and you can't skip up Hatton as you might up Audlem. But you only need one gate at each end with a narrow cruiser, and with a lock-wheeler going ahead you can do the lot easily in 3 hours. The

LLANGOLLEN

LOCK   (WOLVERLEY)

MOTORWAY   (BCN)

NORTHAMPTON ARM

upper part of the flight is a glorious sight in line ahead of you, and when you turn round, you can begin to see Warwick spire apparently lifting itself up as you get higher.

A large building alongside was once a lunatic asylum, if you wish to air your knowledge as you work.

HECK (GREAT)

Whether this place is the origin of the Yorkshire expression 'By Heck!' I don't know, but the village of the name is to be found near the Aire & Calder Navigation. It might pass unnoticed by the canal traveller, but at the side of the waterway is a rare sight for these parts—a harbour full of pleasure boats.

Developed from an old stone-loading basin unused since the middle of the last century, Heck basin is now a haven from Aire & Calder barge washes. It has been vigorously improved by the South Yorkshire Boat Club, which offers a warm welcome, if there is space, to passing canallers. Since overnight moorings are difficult to find along here, and barges seem to sweep by at all hours, Heck must shelter many a thankful boater for the night, safely bedded down without being tossed from his bunk in the middle of dreams.

HIRE BOATS

I've heard irritable boat-owners muttering crossly that all people making their first trip on a hire boat should carry a large 'L' fore and aft; but this is perhaps uncharitable. I'd settle instead for a prominent notice in the cockpit saying THIS BOAT HAS NO BRAKES; for the inability to stop is possibly the chief cause of trouble with beginners, and this state of affairs can cause a lot of harm to somebody else.

Of course, the occasional collisions and confusions on canals are not always due to hire boats, but by the nature of things most people learn their canal cruising in this way. Moreover—and let's be honest—there are some hire boats around which are not either very well designed or very well maintained, as reputable hire

5

firms are the first to agree. So one way and another, hire boats cause a certain amount of nervousness among old-established users of canals.

Well known hire firms, from Canal Pleasurecraft and Anglo-Welsh Cruisers onwards, would readily admit the problems caused by beginners, but they would also point out that some canallers hire boats year after year, and can be counted among the most experienced and considerate canal users in the land. They might also add that responsible firms take a lot of trouble to keep their boats in excellent trim and working condition, which is more than can be said for many casual owners.

Ah well, the debate will continue while ever the channels are narrow! Most boat-owners came to boating through first experiences with hire boats, and canal boat design has certainly benefited from the knowledge of those who build those hire boats. So just as boaters learn to live with anglers, so owners learn to live alongside hirers, even though irritations arise at times; and while many an expert has fumed at many a beginner holding him up at locks, we might also offer thanks to the eager boat-hirers who keep the channels moving in March and October when most private boats are laid up.

HORSES

Horses pulling narrow boats are usually talked about sentimentally as things of the past. Surprisingly, though, they seem to be returning, and horse-boat trips—for short distances anyhow—are being resumed in various places from Llangollen to Berkhamsted. A year or two ago, in fact, a pair of barges with hotel accommodation were pulled up and down the Grand Union for longer cruises, to the astonishment of other boats. As far as I can discover, however, there's only one horse still pulling commercial boats now, and you can spot him on the Birmingham Canal Navigations taking one of those mysterious loads that still seem to travel these strange canals.

The snag about horses now is the decrepit state of the towpaths (see p 136). The horse may not mind the depth of mud on the path in some of the Shroppie cuttings, but on parts of the Oxford, Grand Union, Worcester & Birmingham and other canals there just isn't a towpath at all for yards at a time. There the unfortunate horse would have to take to the hedge.

Now that the fashion for horses is returning, trip-boat operators may like to recall that boats were once pulled by donkeys and

mules, two donkeys equalling one horse. Once the boat is moving, the work isn't too hard these days, and with suitable brightly-painted bobbins to prevent chafing, a new lively attraction could appear on the canals. The rest of us would have to keep ourselves awake, however, to make sure that we always passed on the opposite side to the towline.

ICE

Try cruising in winter—no queues at Foxton, no jamming into Napton locks with a shoehorn, no bouncing off nervous steerers in Wast Hill tunnel, no hopeless search for moorings at the *Wharf* or the *Anchor*, the *Malt Shovel* or the *Navigation*. You have the canals almost to yourself, always provided you've taken a very close look at the stoppage lists before you set out on your journey.

There's just one snag—the water may freeze. This doesn't happen often but it is a possibility, and at times it may stay frozen for weeks, which isn't very funny if you're halfway from somewhere to somewhere. Unless you have a steel boat or a good old-fashioned solid wooden narrow boat, it isn't a good idea to keep moving. The ice may be thin enough for you to crash through, but pieces of ice can have razor edges and in time cut through the hull. I've managed to push through floating ice-floes with strong GRP, but even this can lose its gel coat. I've also seen a man in a GRP boat pushing a bent metal sheet before him as an icebreaker, and charging along quite happily. But with a normal canal cruiser it's better to tie up till it thaws.

This in itself is a problem, for safe moorings are few; and even if you find a helpful boatyard you are still stuck miles away from car, destination, and home. So you find yourself ambling through all kinds of unfamiliar places in a variety of buses and trains before you eventually link everything up, unload the boat, and return home.

Then, of course, you must do it all in reverse to rescue the boat once more. Don't let me put you off, however. Provided you have warm clothing, plenty of blankets, and some form of heating, and provided the temperature stays even slightly above freezing, cruising in winter can be fascinating. You may even meet the ghost of an old icebreaker, pulled by a gang of horses and with a load of men hanging on and rocking furiously.

JUNCTIONS

A junction on a canal is so rare as to be an event, and just as these places were historically interesting when one company met another, so nowadays they are landmarks on a cruise. Most junctions are famous. Hawkesbury was once such a busy rendez-vous for narrow boats that they would stretch along the cut as far as the eye could see. Even in recent years I've had to thread my way gingerly through dozens of them there. The mouth of the Soar, where the Leicester Grand Union faces the Erewash across the Trent, can be like Piccadilly Circus with boats at summer weekends. Stourport and Worcester are startling places where canals meet the Severn through a jumble of basins and locks, heavily cluttered with non-canal boats.

The Grand Union has many junctions along its length—two with the Thames, others at Bulls Bridge, Cowley Peachey, Bulbourne and Marsworth, and the great junctions with the Nene, the Leicester line, the Oxford, the Stratford and eventually the BCN.

Some junctions can be awkward brutes. The one beyond the *Rose and Castle* at Braunston is so sharp and blind that it almost needs traffic lights at times. At Hawkesbury itself a peculiar hairpin turn beyond the lock forces you to run back parallel to your previous route, and there's a similar turn if you come up from the south and want to enter the Caldon Canal. But the oddest junctions are at Hardings Wood and Hazelhurst, for here the Macclesfield and the Leek branch of the Caldon respectively take off on the wrong side, and then cross on aqueducts the very canals they have just left (see FLYOVERS).

As you'd expect, some junctions are popular meeting-places, though it's surprising how few of them seem to have a pub handy. Trent Lock at the start of the Erewash has two, and Fradley has its famous *Swan*, but elsewhere many busy junctions are dry. Some, indeed, are almost isolated. Hurleston, Kings Norton, Marston and even Napton seem cut off from the world, and quite eerie. Yet Barbridge, not far from Hurleston, and Braunston, not far from Napton, have some of the busiest concentrations of boats on the canals.

The most fascinating junctions are in the BCN, where many still remain from the large numbers of the past. The important one at Horsley Fields is almost invisible from the main line, and Factory Junction at Tipton can easily send you off on the Old Line instead of down the three steps to the New. Tame Valley Junction cowers under cooling towers, Brades Hall owns an enjoyable little staircase of two locks, Windmill End sits under Cobb's Engine House at the end of Netherton tunnel, Catshill points you up to Anglesey basin, and Sneyd's hairpin sadly links only with a dry bed now. Farmer's Bridge (see p 52) is the most famous, but Salford Bridge is now the most fantastic. But how about Pudding Green for the most appealing junction in the BCN?

KIDS

You can't travel far without coming across kids—more properly known as children. You see them especially at locks and movable bridges, but they also lean over parapets of fixed bridges, walk along towpaths in organised crocodiles and otherwise, stand in small groups playing ducks and drakes with pebbles, or sit solemnly fishing for all the world like little grown-ups (I saw hundreds of them doing this one day near Gloucester).

Nine out of ten of them are quite harmless, and indeed positively helpful at times. Some are extremely interested in canals, knowledgeable about them, and willing recipients of your pontificatings. Their most embarrasing fault is an eagerness to help you, particularly at locks, and you have to make some sort of a decision about this. Do you shoo them hastily away for safety reasons, or do you let them swarm over the gates and balance-beams like rabbits, to the danger of your blood pressure?

I've never been sure of the right answer. Unless they're obvious trouble-makers I think it's wrong to drive them away, but you can get terribly pompous if you start ordering them about and issuing solemn warnings. Some kids, in fact, turn out to be highly skilled in operating locks. I tend, then, to apply three general rules with the normal children who really do want to help. I keep them on the right side of the balance-beams (to save them from being swept in); I don't let them stay on moving gates (although they love it); and I rarely hand over a windlass (I lose enough myself).

A reasonable mixture of friendliness and firmness seems to ensure their cooperation, and you may have made them canal addicts for life. Beware of the rather smarter lads here and there who offer their services for hire or reward, especially at swing bridges on the Leeds & Liverpool. I don't have many dealings with these, though there's a useful lad appears at the Wigan flight at times. We usually carry a bag of sweets, however, for the non-mercenary ones, who are often delighted. I've even given a lift to a couple of hitchhiking young fishermen who were far from home (but not, I fear, to the urchins at Smethwick locks who rudely demanded one).

There are other urchins in my remaining 10 per cent, and they are among the minor menaces of canal cruising, especially in built-up areas such as the BCN. They idly drop handfuls of gravel from bridges, or fling grit from behind bushes. In extreme cases they throw stones and break windows. Their least harmful, but most revolting, variation is to spit down on you as you shoot a bridge, but luckily they are rotten shots.

The best kids of all are, of course, the ones you know; they usually make excellent crew members from quite an early age. They take to canalling like ducks to water, and in no time are working you up Hatton as fast as you can leap on and off the boat. I really couldn't have written this book without some of them.

LADDERS

Ladders can sometimes serve a useful purpose, especially if, like me, you sometimes go cruising on your own. Sooner or later, as in the Wigan flight, for example, you will find yourself at the bottom of a lock which is too deep to clamber out of, and this is where a ladder comes into its own.

Most locks, luckily, drop only about 6 ft, and most people can scramble from the roof of the boat on to the lock side. But there are quite a few 8- and 9-footers about, and when you come to the 10-, 11- and 12-footers of the Trent & Mersey, the Staffs & Worcs, and Wigan—not to mention the 14-footer at Tardebigge —you would need suction-pads to climb the cliff-like sides.

Canal-builders, no doubt, expected one person to do the lock work and one to stay on the boat, but many wives whose husbands insist on doing the steering don't go along with this. Thus many a steerer, after sliding into the lock, has to leave the boat and wrestle with the paddle-gear. And here and there, nowadays, he'll find ladders at the sides of some of the deep locks.

At Stenson, for example (and now, I'm glad to see, at Weston and Swarkestone), there's a very welcome ladder let into the

lock side, and you can take your ropes and windlass in your teeth and shin smartly up it before the boat drifts across to the other side of the wide lock. In some of the Leeds & Liverpool locks the ladders have been added at a later stage and protrude from the lock side, and many a boat must have hit them as it entered. Moreover, some of them are on the opposite side to the bollards, preventing you from shinning up and tying the boat up in these wide locks. If you reach the River Weaver, by the way, there are some fascinating ladders consisting merely of foot-holes and hand-holds instead of rungs.

There are plenty of deep locks, however, with no built-in ladders, and here I find a light portable one worth more than its weight in gold. I hop on to the roof with the ladder in one hand, lodge it securely against the grab-rail at the bottom, and nip up it. This has to be done pretty quickly, for although in a narrow lock the boat can't leave the lock side, it can move forwards or backwards, taking the ladder with it. So it's one-two-up, and a quick grab back to whip the ladder on to the lock side.

I missed this last movement once at Hurleston when the lock-keeper put up a paddle and I had to attend to my ropes smartly, but I did learn that my ladder floated. Certainly, if you ever go canalling on your own, one of these light aluminium ladders can save you the laborious job of heaving your boat in and out of locks—especially when you have to lie on your stomach at some of those tail-end footbridges.

LIFT-BRIDGES see MOVING BRIDGES

LLANGOLLEN

All the best travel articles rave about this canal, thus filling it so full of boats that the writers sabotage their own eulogies. Everybody starts on the Llangollen; some must vow never to return.

Boatyards cluster like flies near it. I've even heard boats roaring up the Shropshire Union all night in order to get to it. The result is that for much of the summer there may be queues at the entrance locks and then milling muddles at the very narrow length near Llangollen itself.

It's a pleasant enough canal if you can keep away from the rush hours, though the finest part comprises only the last few miles. Here the two great aqueducts and the mountains of Wales are certainly worth cruising—preferably in March or November.

LOCK COTTAGES

This is a sad subject. At one time there were lock houses along waterways from one end to the other. Each canal company built to its own design, from the famous barrel-roofed cottages on part of the Stratford to the squat buildings on the Shropshire

Union, from the tall overhanging-roofed cottages at the tops of Foxton and Northampton flights to the solid, grim, clearly numbered boxes of the BCN.

Often these houses had bay windows, presumably so that the keeper could see both ways down the canal. None of them to my mind, apart perhaps from the Stratford barrels, are as intriguing as the pillared bridge-keepers' houses on the Gloucester-Sharpness.

Anyhow, in recent years they've all been falling down fast,

so that the click of my camera has hardly died away before the subject of its photograph has passed into history. At Atherstone, Claydon and Kings Norton, and at dozens of other places, there are now mounds of rubble or mere empty spaces where lock houses used to be. It would take an archaeologist to discover traces of some of them, but useful clues are a tangled lilac bush in bloom, the coloured waterfall of a rambler rose, or a gnarled old apple tree; for the gardens fight on though the houses are gone.

No doubt the pleasant shapes of so many of these cottages failed to make up for their remoteness from roads and services. No doubt, too, the constant diminishing of the labour force caused houses to empty, and then they were set on by vandals or officially destroyed. Luckily, though, some of those that remain have been restored by enthusiasts who prefer to live peacefully alongside a canal rather than murderously alongside a road. So let's raise our hats to the lock-keepers who soldier on, and to the people who keep lock cottages alive.

LOCK-KEEPERS

These men, once members of a common species, are now becoming rare; in some places they have been re-christened Water Controllers. They lived where there are now often mounds of rubble near locks (see LOCK COTTAGES). They used to coddle their locks with loving care, referee fights between boatmen in a hurry, and wield their kebs to remove rubbish, as well as working well into the night when needed.

Some of those who remain still mow their slopes and lock sides with pride, grease their paddle-gear, give a helping hand to mystified beginners, and tell hair-raising tales of emptying pounds, hung-up boats, smashed paddle-racks and lost windlasses. At busy lock flights such as Wigan, Audlem, Napton and Lapworth you still see them around, though cheerful 'Matey' no longer pedals furiously down Northampton; but oddly enough I have yet to see one at Tardebigge or Hatton, though obviously they have passed that way.

If there are ghosts in canal tunnels, there must, surely, be hundreds of ghostly lock-keepers among the 1317 usable locks of our inland waterways.

LOCK NAMES

There's Big at Middlewich, Odd at Wootton Wawen, Quoisley and Povey's on the Llangollen, Rumps on the Trent & Mersey, Hell Meadow at Wigan, Stegneck at Gargrave and lots of Old

Fords in the East End—all of them lock names. Just take a look at the Staffs & Worcs Canal, which has Bumblehole and Stewponey, Bratch and Dimmingsdale, Wightwick and Awebridge, Falling Sands and Boggs, Filance and Tixall—names rivalling or matching the bridge names on this canal in as intriguing a mixture of comedy and poetry as you could hope to find anywhere.

The Upper Avon, however, has hit on a different idea. You pass instead through the Robert Aickman Lock, the Inland Waterways Association Lock, and the W. A. Cadbury Lock. The idea of naming locks after the benefactors or inspirers of this magnificent restoration is understandable, but somehow these names fail to trip happily from cruising tongues, and it might not be advisable for future restorations to continue the practice. Carthagena Lock or Hoo Mill Lock is fine, but names like the Lower Puddlecombe Women's Institute Lock, or the Battersea Plastic Bottle & Bicycle Pump Manufacturing Co's Lock, though worthy, should be eschewed.

LOCKS

There are all kinds of references to locks elsewhere in this book, but a general mention may not be amiss. Millions of words must have been spoken and written about these contraptions, and much confusion must have resulted. What are locks, when you come to think about them?

They are merely boxes of water straddling your route, with the canal at one end of them higher up than the canal at the other. They have holes at each end that can be covered or uncovered to let water in or out. Thus you can have the lock water at the same level as the canal at either of its ends. The boxes also have doors at each end (which we have to learn to call gates), and these can only be opened at one end at any given time because of the water pressure (yes, I know about Sawley Flood Lock and those others on the Soar and elsewhere). Of course, the gates can't be opened at all unless the water on each side of them is at the same level.

So by uncovering the right openings we bring the lock water to the level that our boat is at outside the gate, then open the gate to let the boat in. We shut the gate, close its openings, and open the holes at the other end (see GATE-PADDLES, GROUND PADDLES, COGS AND CATCHES, WIND-LASSES, SIDE PONDS, etc, etc). The water in the lock and the boat then rise up or down as the case may be, until they've both reached the level of the next length of waterway. Gates open, boat out, gates closed, openings covered—all done.

Clear as mud, really. But how fascinatingly varied are the permutations and combinations of these incredible devices, whether in their gates, paddle-gear, balance-beams, footplanks, bollards, ladders or even basic shapes! Even more fascinating are the ways in which different crews set about the job of tackling a lock! I'm surprised they haven't tried Harry Worth in a whole television series based on this seemingly simple task.

MIDDLE LEVEL

It's unfair to leave out the Middle Level Drains from any book about canals, for although they are not officially navigations, they are undoubtedly artificial waterways; and they certainly carry boats. So if you ever wish to cruise below sea level in a remarkable collection of waters far from the crowds, try these.

You reach them from the canals via the Nene past Peterborough, forking right to Stanground Sluice. You negotiate a narrow channel and an awkward bend at Whittlesey, drop further through Ashline lock, and you're there.

The Canals Book gives you details of fees for the Nene, and how to organise your trip into the Middle Level. You must give notice to the Commissioners, and you'll meet shallow places and weed. But you'll also meet enthusiasts in March, and, with perhaps some hauling and weed-clearing, you may even tackle Horseway Sluice and Welches Dam lock with its curious paddle-gear; and you may nip through Salters Lode when the tide is right and through Denver to the Great Ouse system.

The scenery isn't very spectacular because you can't see it most of the time, but these weird waterways are undoubtedly memorable.

MILEPOSTS

Rare nowadays, except perhaps on the Trent & Mersey and the Leeds & Liverpool, are the mileposts that once punctuated canal journeys.

The best time to see those that remain is in spring, before the vegetation hides them, and it's quite surprising how many you find then. Those along the Leeds & Liverpool are not very attractive, being more like road milestones, but they crop up fairly regularly, marking the distances from each end of the canal. Because the total distance is $127\frac{1}{4}$ miles, the Leeds distance

always has the odd $\frac{1}{4}$-mile tacked on to it. Curiously, unlike road mileposts, the distance from each town is given on the side facing that town.

Undoubtedly the most attractive posts are on the Shropshire Union, though few and far between. Mostly they are blue with white lettering and contain three panels—giving the distances to Nantwich, Autherley and Norbury. They're a fair weight, too, as I found when I tried to lift one displaced by contractors. The Brecon & Abergavenny could only afford small numbered plates, leaving you to guess what the number refers to, but the Trent & Mersey has tall and solid metal posts clearly sorting out the 92 miles between Preston Brook and Shardlow. Similar posts on its Caldon branch amusingly still give the distance to Uttoxeter, which has long since lost any trace of a canal. There is even one by the railway that replaced this canal length.

The rarest mileposts are perhaps the old Grand Junction signs on the Leicester—pleasant oblong plates giving the mileage to Leicester itself. But the oddest post of all is a Trent & Mersey one, let into the pavement by the *Longboat* pub at Farmer's Bridge in the middle of Birmingham. Why this was allowed to leave its proper place and turn up by a waterway that has nothing to do with it is a mystery.

MOORING

In theory you can moor for a night, a meal, shopping or a snooze anywhere on the towpath side, except at locks and bridges, but in fact this doesn't always work out. On the Shroppie, the Oxford, the Staffs & Worcs and even the Grand Union nowadays you can try for miles to get anywhere near the towpath, without success. Lengths of edging have fallen in and generations of engines, together with today's minority of canal cowboys, have washed in the silt—and there is no money available to dig it out again. So unless you carry a gangplank or are prepared to jump, you must keep on nosing in or probing with a shaft until you find a deep enough spot. But beware when bringing your propeller end in, even then.

Impatient boaters don't bother with all this, but tie up at the deeper places just above locks, where bollards and dredging are intended for others wishing to work the lock. So as you hopefully cruise up to land your crew armed with windlasses, you find some selfish fellow moored there and sunbathing on the roof or gone shopping. This situation is specially troublesome if you are cruising on your own, for you can't secure the boat to go and wind the paddles. These lock-bollard hoggers have even been known to leave their boats encumbering lock entrances for weeks, and unworthy thoughts of casting off their lines and letting them drift must have entered many heads.

There's an odd thing about night moorings. However remote

the spot you choose, within 5 minutes, as often as not, somebody else will tie up a yard from you, and then somebody else, and then somebody else. Are they frightened of the cows, the silence, the dawn chorus, or the ghost of Kit Crewbucket? Or can it be that today's motorist, used to being hemmed in by other cars all the time, is terrified to park alone when on a boat?

Permanent moorings bring out two curious attitudes among boaters. First, people seem to be willing to pay many hundreds of pounds for a boat but begrudge paying for a safe mooring, and thus tie it to the nearest tree. Second, it is fashionable to decry 'marina' as a dirty word on canals, and to object to these tidily kept gatherings of hundreds of boats. The result of these two attitudes may well be endless ribbons of moored boats from Little Venice to Ripon and from Boston to Llangollen—a quarter of them sunk or sinking through neglect, abandonment or vandalism. But gather them neatly in supervised marinas and actually pay rent—never!

On a happier note, however, what can be a pleasanter sound than the ring of a hammer on a mooring spike, heard up and down the canals as boats moor for the night? But never put your hammer down in the grass, and never drop your mooring pins on the deck, for they bounce.

MOTORWAYS

In an odd way motorways have impinged surprisingly on canals since the M1 first reached out towards Birmingham, though they haven't bothered us much yet. The most obvious meeting places are where the roads have had to cross the canals. Instead of simple weathered bridges we find ourselves cruising through great echoing concrete tunnels, such as the one on the way down the Northampton flight, or where the Staffs & Worcs burrows under the M6 near Penkridge. The bridge builders were generous, and made broad platforms at the sides of the water that are often used by farmers as free shelters for animals. The concrete walls, of course, are used freely by the ubiquitous scrawlers and wielders of aerosol paint-sprays.

NARROW BOAT   (CALDON)

POWER STATION   (RUGELEY)

ROPE MARKS   (PERRY BARR)

The most remarkable contact between canals and motorways is in the Black Country, where there seems to be so much derelict land alongside the waterways that it has automatically attracted the road planners. So now the BCN explorer is often in sight of a motorway, and sometimes actually running alongside or weaving about under one.

There are two extraordinary places in this Black Country motorway/canal complex. First is the famous Spaghetti Junction, which so many motorists talk of with awe because of the different levels of road and because they can easily go 20 miles out of their way if they take a wrong fork. But what they don't know is that under this lot lies a canal crossroads, where the Birmingham-Fazeley passes the ends of both the Grand Union and the Tame Valley canals, and under the canals, to finish it all off, runs the River Tame.

When all the motorways and their stilts were being built, the contractors had to move a temporary bridge by means of a huge crane every time a boat came along. I enjoyed this simple feeling of power several times. Now, of course, the canals wriggle peacefully under a forest of great concrete legs.

The second striking place on the BCN is near Oldbury. Here the Old Line between Birmingham and Wolverhampton swung round over the New Line on an aqueduct, with a sort of slip road down Spon Lane locks connecting the two, and a railway running alongside to complete the mixture. Now the motorway, using the tempting ground available, has soared almost exactly over everything.

Looking up from the New Line you can see the railway above and, to the side of you, both rail and New Line crossed by the Old Line, and the whole collection now topped by the motorway on criss-cross legs—a selection of transport routes all coming together at the same place.

The Old Line in particular meanders for some distance under the motorway, which provides effective shelter from the rain. You can even moor under it for the night and hardly hear a thing.

The links between waterways and motorways are not always friendly. Regularly there are threats of new motorways flattening

6

canals as indeed the M6 did south of Kendal. So cruise under the next motorway happily, but keep your eyes skinned for any plans for new ones.

MOVING BRIDGES

The cheapest way of bridging a canal must have been to put the bridge just above water level and arrange for it to be movable. This saved a lot of work, and cut down on materials needed in building up approach embankments and a permanent crossing at a higher level, not to mention dispersing with the towpath underneath for the horse. So in different parts of the system you'll come across bridges which you have to move out of your way, either upwards or sideways.

The simplest one I know is at the Maidboats yard at Brinklow, where somebody usually swings a small footbridge (almost invisible) out of the way as you nervously tackle the narrow channel. There's a similar little footbridge that lifts up as you pass through Cadbury's at Bournville on the Worcester & Birmingham. Most movable bridges, however, are for vehicles, and they range from simple farm crossings to great electrically operated contraptions on busy roads, as in Liverpool, and even to a swung railway bridge on the Aire & Calder.

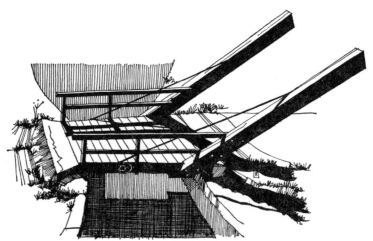

The lift-up bridges are found in greatest abundance on the Oxford, the Llangollen, the Caldon and the Brecon & Abergavenny. You pull down a simple low-level angled beam on the Oxford, and a high-level beam on the others, in order to raise the platform of the bridge at an angle to the water. Then whoever is driving the boat must slide precariously through, with an eye on the paint-marked underbeams of the bridge.

The bridges that swing sideways are less harassing for steerers, but sometimes more infuriating for the bridge-opener. There are many of these on the Leeds & Liverpool, usually easy to swing with the aid of an arm to get hold of and an eye for oncoming road traffic. But on the Rufford Branch, on the upper Peak Forest, and sometimes on the Macclesfield, swing-bridges have been known to turn many a face purple.

There are odd self-operated swing-bridges elsewhere—on the Coventry and the Grand Union, for example—and those who tackle the fascinatingly revived Avon will find a few across some locks there. The most memorable, however, are those on some larger canals, for here they often swing themselves open as you approach.

These bridges are honoured by having bridge-keepers, who on the Aire & Calder either press buttons or go round and round as if pressing cider, at the end of long capstan arms. On the Gloucester-Sharpness they pop out of their remarkable little houses and turn handles that carry them round on the bridge as it swings. On both these canals they have you taped as you cruise along, and almost always swing into action before you need to sound your horn.

The crew-operated moving bridges often have characters of their own, and the lifting ones especially must be treated with respect. Don't think Wrenbury, for example, is going to stay up for you after lifting, as do most of the others on the Llangollen—if you turn your back, you'll find it's on its way down again—and on the Oxford also you never know. Some bridges stay up, but others need a burly crew member to sit on the beam. So beware of tempting offers from child gongoozlers, especially in Banbury.

NARROW BOATS

I nervously mention the converted versions under NODDY BOATS, so here let me stay on the safer ground of the genuine commercial carrying boats, where the first, which has a motor, tows the second, the butty, which has no motor.

Unhappily, these are rarer and rarer sights. Not many years ago they could be seen regularly on the Coventry, the northern Oxford and the Grand Union, where Blue Line and Willow Wren, and later individual enthusiasts, slogged on with cargoes of coal to London or grain to Wellingborough. The Brays and the Collinses, *Belmont* and *Raymond*, *Ash* and *Comet*, and many other well known people and boats were familiar sights.

Some of these and others also ventured elsewhere, and there was an encouraging oil-carrying run from Ellesmere Port to Aldridge, and even a cargo of timber over the Leeds & Liverpool to Leicester. Now almost all these runs are gone, and like the cocoa boats of earlier years the boats themselves are lying scattered or converted in many places.

All is not over. You may still meet the occasional cargo in surprising places, and there are even enthusiasts loading their boats with coal and selling it by the bag wherever their fancy takes them on the cut. But there's an air of resignation about, and when you see a Narrow Boat Trust being formed to preserve examples of commercial boats, the sad implication is only too obvious.

This is a miserable story. Despite the limitations of our narrow locks and shallow channels compared with the much more capacious canals on the Continent, there could surely still have been a place for these colourful and beautifully kept boats in the carrying trade. There must be something or other that doesn't need to be rushed murderously along our overcrowded roads. But of course the fundamental trouble is that our canals were never bold and wide enough and incredibly no British government has ever had the sense to do something about it. Maybe the Common Market will at last bring us some real commercial canals such as our European colleagues have, if only to stop them laughing at us.

NETHERTON TUNNEL

There are many tunnels, but only one Netherton. It doesn't quite take the record for the longest tunnel, though at 3,027 yd it's a large hole, but it was the last tunnel dug on our canals (1858), and it is also the widest.

It is one of the two tunnels linking the network of northern and central canals of the BCN with the lengths of Dudley Canal and the Stourbridge in the south-west. The incredible warren of the original Dudley Tunnel, 3,172 yd, was becoming a bottleneck with its one-way working and its subsidence troubles, so this new link was dug under the hills parallel to it and just over a mile away, on the same level as the Birmingham New Line, which it joined at Dudley Port.

It has, unusually, a towpath on either side—which you'll find makes steering more puzzling. At one time it had lights, and tolls were originally paid to help to cover the cost of digging in this unstable soil. Going through Netherton now does seem like passing between two different worlds, and as soon as you emerge at the northern end you pass under the Old Line of the BCN before joining the New Line. At Dudley Port you are already on an embankment from which you can look back at the ridge of hills you've just burrowed through.

NODDY BOATS

This is a delicate subject, originally belonging to those unhappy realms of narrow-boats-versus-the-rest controversy—a theme still kept alive by a few fanatics who seem to have invented the term 'noddy boat' to describe almost any kind of canal boat which isn't a full-size narrow boat complete with bearded crew. It has now dawned on them that there were increasing numbers of canal enthusiasts who didn't want, or couldn't afford, to lumber themselves with 70 ft of boat for three or four people; and it even became obvious that this growing number of 'non-narrow-boaters' could be fighters just as devoted to the canal cause and just as careful in their use of the canals as the traditionalists.

It seems that the real devotees have eventually formed a slightly uneasy alliance, whether they cruise in canoes or full-size lock-fillers, against an even newer tribe of canal cowboys, who flit up and down the waterways on fine weekends. Their boats may be small like those of many true enthusiasts, but their engines are usually bigger, and they roar to the nearest pub, upsetting everyone's cup of tea and fishing lines in the process (see WASH).

These, I believe, are the 'noddy boaters' now. They care little for the peace of the canals, they join no Inland Waterways Association, they smash the paddle-gear on the rare occasions when they use locks, they ruin the peaceful mooring, fishing or walking of others, and it's really not quite clear why they are on the canals at all. They would obviously be happier flaunting themselves just off the beach at Brighton, or doing 90 mph up the outside lane of a motorway.

Fortunately their numbers are small, perhaps because they discover that canals are not quite as easy to use as they thought. They are fine-weather boaters anyhow, and you can always get away from them by heading for the nearest collection of locks.

NOISES

No handbook mentions the noises you will hear on canals, but these are among the most noticeable things to newcomers. The most startling fact, however, is the silence, especially after driving to the boat. There is never absolute silence, of course, for even when the engine has stopped there is always a bird somewhere, and up in the bows of a longish boat there is the somnolent ripple of water to hide even the distant engine.

There are faint tractor noises at times, with tiny clatters of haybalers in summer and combine harvesters later. Sheep make silly noises, though cows usually stay quiet. But these are noises of the country anywhere, except that they are drowned when you're in a car.

It is the noises peculiar to canals that stay in the memory. The most musical is the ring of paddle-gear as a rack rises and plays its tune on the ratchet (it is less musical if it is dropped by some anti-social show-off). You can hear paddle-gear noises over long distances on still days, a sure sign that there's a boat working its way towards you.

Another musical sound, which I have mentioned elsewhere, is the tune of the hammer on the mooring spike as it drives it into the reluctant towpath. This also sounds for long distances in the quiet of evening as boats settle down for the night.

The most nostalgic canal noise, though, is the phut-phut-phut of a narrow boat engine. Strong men weep at this sound, which has become rare as the commercial narrow boats have thinned out. Luckily, addicts go to extraordinary lengths to keep such engines chugging, so that the distant noise is just as likely to be a beautifully fitted out conversion these days instead of a pair of loaded boats.

NORTHAMPTON ARM

This 5-mile stretch of narrow canal deserves a mention for several reasons. It's a strenuous bit of exercise for a start, with seventeen locks between the Grand Union and Northampton (including one almost under the concrete tunnel of the M1). There are intriguing lift-bridges, the wild remains of one-time lock-cottage gardens, a gloomy old factory and wharf just before Northampton, and at the end of it all you drop down to the magnificent River Nene, ready to wind its watermeadow way through all those great guillotine locks down to Peterborough and the Middle Level.

So don't pass by Gayton Junction if you're ever up the Grand Union. Turn off if your boat is narrow enough, and help to keep this fascinating stretch of canal in use.

NOTICES

Besides the 'extraordinary weights', or dangerously vague 'ordinary traffic of the district' mentioned under BRIDGE NOTICES, there are other interesting notices here and there as you cruise along. On the Llangollen, for example, you are warned in solid iron that you must tip your load of stone 5 ft away from the water's edge.

SIDE PONDS   (KNOWLE)

SILL   (LOUGHBOROUGH)

SPLIT BRIDGE   (TRENT AND MERSEY)

STOURPORT

STAIRCASES   (TWO AT STOURPORT)

TUNNEL   (BARNTON)

TURF LOCK   (KENNET AND AVON)

The Llangollen and the Shroppie are busy providers of notices, in fact. You are not to moor over the stop grooves under the bridge where the arm goes to Ellesmere, and I was pleased to see an unusually sensible notice at Grindley Brook saying 'Please wind paddles down to prevent damage. Don't let them drop', as well as another heart-cry saying 'Please do not tie up to this water tap'. There are some smart new notices nowadays at swing-bridges, hopefully warning unauthorised persons not to touch them, and some rather older notices screwed to lock beams to exhort us to work the locks properly to avoid draining

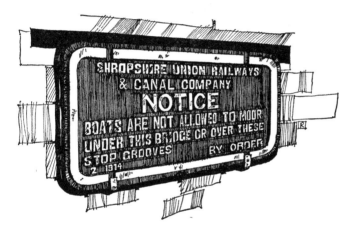

the pounds. More fleeting are the sheets of paper periodically pasted up to warn people against trespassing, throwing in rubbish, etc. These have a sadly short life: some I noticed being pasted up all over the BCN once were still there a few months later, but the print had faded to illegibility wherever they faced the sun.

The oddest notice I know is one marking a 'Prize Length' near Appley Bridge on the Leeds & Liverpool. Presumably this was to encourage the lengthsmen, but are there others anywhere? The most puzzling to most canallers are those huge blue notices erected a few years ago announcing to passing trains the identity of various canals, together with a Leeds telephone number for passengers to call. The exact purpose of these expensive sheets of metal has always eluded us, and we should dearly love to know just how many passengers leap out at the other end and ring up Leeds. And what do they say when they get through?

There may be some publicity value, but I've often heard the comment that the cost of these large notices would be better spent on dredgers. Hooligans with air guns seem to think the same thing.

OUTBOARDS AND OUTDRIVES see ENGINES, POLYTHENE BAGS

PADDLE-GEAR see COGS AND CATCHES, GATE-PADDLES, GROUND PADDLES, LOCKS, SIDE PONDS, WINDLASSES

POLYTHENE BAGS

One of the technological wonders of our times is polythene, but its assets are unhappily counterbalanced by its drawbacks, the chief of which is indestructibility. Thus, when it is discarded, it lives on endlessly, drifting happily about the countryside.

It brings itself especially to our notice on the canals in the form of fertiliser bags. The contents are used in vast quantities on farms nowadays, and the bags then drift into the nearest canal. There—blue, green and yellow—they lurk just below the surface, waiting for our innocent propellers. They wrap themselves securely round these, effectively stopping the engine or breaking a shear-pin, and often causing further damage.

It is then necessary to cut them off, preferably with a bread knife, and standing on one's head or even wading in the water. It is here that users of outboard engines or outdrives come into their own, since with these the cocooned propeller can be lifted clear of the water.

Anti-social canallers, in a temper, throw the remains on the bank, or even into the water again. More responsible persons bury them or take them home.

PONTCYSYLLTE

Don't ask me how you pronounce this; ask a Welshman. I've seen it spelt in different ways, too, and different people seem to have different ideas as to how many pillars and arches it has. At least everyone seems to be agreed that it is one of the most spectacular achievements, sights, and experiences of the whole canal system, and that crossing it is either highly exciting or highly terrifying, according to your temperament.

Pontcysyllte is, of course, the famous aqueduct just over the Welsh border, where the Llangollen Canal suddenly decides to turn smartly and leap across the Dee valley. If the original plans had gone through, we should have been deprived of this remarkable structure. The idea at first was to step down three locks at each end and cross on a much less dominating aqueduct of stone, with only three arches. Indeed, work started on quarrying the stone for this purpose. But Jessop, under whom Telford had by then been appointed, suddenly proposed a much higher and longer crossing without locks, and in an iron trough on seven great arches.

Well, we can see it now, not on seven but on nineteen arches, held up by eighteen pillars—and if the arithmetic looks wrong there, it's because the outer ends of the first and the last arch rest on land. The trough of iron is 1,007 ft long, and the highest point of the aqueduct above low water in the Dee is 121 ft. The first 70 ft of the tall piers is solid, but above that they are hollow. The arches themselves are of cast iron, and the trough is a mixture of iron plates—418 altogether forming the walls. The canal is 11 ft 10 in wide, and a towpath hangs over it, supported by iron pillars in the water. There's a railing at the outside of the towpath, but nothing at all on the other side of the water channel except the edge of the trough.

Everyone is so staggered by the aqueduct that they entirely overlook the huge embankment, now well disguised by trees, on the approach from the south. This itself was an enormous undertaking in those days, for it stretches for 1,500 ft and is 97 ft above

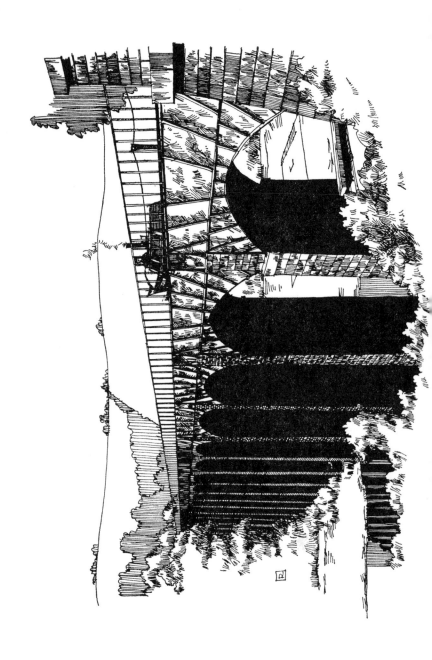

the original ground level before it hands over to the first arch of the aqueduct.

All these figures to a boater, of course, add up to an approach from the south with a sudden view on your right of the great channel striding over empty space. Then after an awkward lift-bridge you turn right and prepare to cross—always provided there isn't already a boat coming in the other direction. A normal narrow canal boat fits the channel almost like a hand in a glove, and if there's any kind of cross wind you are bound to grind your way over. On the side away from the towpath all you can see is thin air, unless you lean well over to make sure that the lip of the iron trough is still keeping the water in. But of course you can hop out on the other side and walk along while your boat faithfully follows you. Then at last you reach the other side, with a friendly boatyard on your right and the much narrower beautiful remaining few miles to Llangollen in front of you.

There's no argument about it, crossing Pontcysyllte is the experience of a lifetime, especially in a gale. It opened in 1805 with cannons firing, but how many more boats must rub against the side of this incredible iron trough before it begins to wear thin?

POWER STATIONS

I must mention these structures, for there are times when you can't get away from them. Up the Trent and along the Trent & Mersey, for example, you're rarely without a stack of cooling towers alongside you—and behind and ahead of you as well. At Ocker Hill and Birchills in the BCN, too, these towers beckon you as you work down Ryder's Green and up Walsall locks respectively. There's Stourport at the end of the Staffs & Worcs, Wigan where the Leigh Branch comes into the Leeds & Liverpool, and I sometimes imagine I spotted some towers mixed up with the oil tanks at Ellesmere Port, but I'm not sure.

The most magnificent of these latter-day canal landmarks is Willington on the Trent & Mersey, seen after dark. Lit up, it's like an enormous Christmas tree or a static firework display, and it will thrill or horrify you as you creep by.

PUBS

Presumably in the old days narrow boats would be moored at pubs along the way rather as cars are now—or perhaps more like lorries at transport cafés. Locking was thirsty work, and after engines came along there was also the job of hauling the butty down a flight by hand. Many of the old canal inns must have disappeared now, but quite a few remain; and though some of them disdainfully ignore the waterway at the bottom of their garden in favour of cars all the year, others welcome boats.

Probably the best known canal pub is the *Rose and Castle* at Braunston, which has had mooring bollards for many years, and has now added an enormous boat-shaped restaurant that must make many of the old boatmen of Braunston turn in their graves (many modern ones, for that matter, have been seen to shudder). Even the *Rose and Castle*, however, with as canally a name at as canally a spot as you could ever hope for, needs its main road trade as well, especially in the winter. There must be very few pubs left that can now look chiefly to the water for their custom.

Cars must have quite a job, however, to find the *Anchor* on the Shropshire Union, the *Globe* near Linslade, and the *Pyewipe* on the Fossdyke, all of which face waterways that must once have brought them most of their trade.

Many of the pub names reveal their origins. I can think of a dozen *Navigations* straight off, from Kilby to Blackburn, from Whaley Bridge to Gnosall, from Bridge 64 on the Grand Union to Gathurst under M6; and there are actually three of them waiting for the lower Peak Forest and the Ashton to reopen, as well as another waiting for the Montgomeryshire at Maesbury. There are *Boats* at Penkridge, Stockton, Thrupp, Loughborough, Newbold, Brewood, and many other places, as well as *Two Boats* at Long Itchington, *Packets* at Dogdyke and on the Chesterfield, a *Packet Boat* on the Lancaster, and of course the modern *Longboat* in the middle of Birmingham. There are *Barges* of one sort or another at Woolhampton, Rodley and Hertford basin, though the first is a *Row Barge*, the second the *Rodley Barge*, and the third an *Old Barge*. There is, however, a plain *Barge* by

Bridge 83 on the Grand Union. On top of all these there are odd *Pleasure Boats*, *Ships*, and a *Paddington Packet Boat* about the place.

There are masses of *Bridges*, too, from Branston near Burton to Etruria by Wedgwood's factory, from Silsden on the Leeds & Liverpool to Audlem on the Shroppie. *Anchors* seem a bit out of place, but there they are, at Hartshill and Glascote, Johnson's Hillock and Salterforth, Bridge 42 on the Shroppie and Bridge 71 on the Staffs & Worcs, with an *Anchor and Hope* on the Lee and Stort. *Wharf* pubs spread from Nuneaton to Congleton, and there are *Swans* everywhere. *Locks* are rarer, but I recall the *Lock* at Wolverley, *Big Lock* and *Kings Lock*, both at Middlewich, the *Lock Vaults* at Chester, and appropriately the *Top Lock* at Wigan. Also appropriately there's an *Aqueduct* at Pontcysyllte, but inappropriately nowadays a *Junction* at Norbury.

The *Jolly Tar* at Barbridge lacks the canal atmosphere, and the *Cape of Good Hope* near Warwick and the *Rock of Gibraltar* on the Oxford seem far from home. Of course, there are lots of normal pub names, which for some reason seem to be dominated by *Red Lions*, with a few *Black* ones thrown in.

I must cease this seemingly alcoholic meander lest, like the compilers of the new British Waterways *Guides*, I appear to suggest that canalling is merely a pub-crawl. In fact pubs are often rare, some canals being less endowed than others. Why this should be so I leave to other earnest researchers. My own plea is for publicans to extend their welcome to canallers, and even, like the *Boat* at Thrupp and the *Navigation* at Wootten Wawen— but very few others—to hang out an attractive canal-flavoured sign for all to see.

RESERVOIRS see SUMMIT LEVELS

RISERS see STAIRCASES

ROPE MARKS

Among the most striking sights when canalling are the deep grooves made by the towropes of the ages. You spot them everywhere if your eyes are open—long, angled ones in the softer stones of some lock sides, a dozen or more at different heights on the corners of some bridges, and, almost incredibly, many more on the metal balustrades of towpath bridges at junctions such as Bordesley in the BCN.

The constant wearing of brick and stone was obviously a worry to canal companies, for the bridge corners on many canals are protected by great metal pillars which themselves have acquired deep grooves. These grooves appeared, of course, only when the horse had to walk at such an angle that the rope rubbed against something. There is even a metal post on a ground paddle in the Perry Barr flight of the BCN that looks as if it has been filed in several places with a giant file; countless thousands of ropes must have strained alongside it.

These rope grooves take one back to the past more startlingly than anything else on the waterways, for they shout so convincingly of the myriads of boats that must have laboured by to produce them.

ROVING BRIDGES see TOWPATHS

RUBBING-STRAKES see FENDERS

RUBBISH DISPOSAL

Since food on a cruise tends to come largely out of tins, packets or polythene, your boat soon acquires a large collection of rubbish. Unfortunately few boat designers seem to incorporate rubbish bins, so various substitutes have to suffice, from bags hanging behind doors to whisky or detergent boxes in the cockpit. Lined up alongside these there is also a growing rank of milk bottles and deposit bottles.

There comes a time when all this gets in the way or begins to smell, and there is an urgent search for dustbins. Officially these appear at frequent intervals, as shown on the cruising charts. But only too often they are either (a) full, (b) hidden, (c) in-

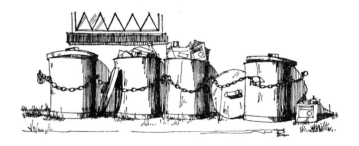

accessible because of other boats, and/or obviously being used by every Tom, Dick and Harry in the neighbourhood. Moreover, there may be a complicated system whereby you have to set to and sort your rubbish into various components and burn one lot in an incinerator, in which a previous visitor has just placed a large mound of wet cabbage leaves.

It is the apparently permanent *fullness* of some dustbins which is the greatest irritation and mystery. Yet, I suppose, it is a bit hard on the local ratepayers to have to finance the removal of rubbish from a lot of passing strangers. One can almost forgive the despairing canallers who start private rubbish dumps at demolished lock houses, in former stables, or in disused sideponds.

7

The Oxford Canal has interesting examples of unofficial dumps, buzzing with fat healthy flies.

SEWAGE WORKS

The less said about these the better, but isn't it odd how often they appear alongside canals? Any protest about this to the authorities is always met by piously raised hands and firm assertions that nothing but pure water enters the canal at any time. Anyone cruising past, say, Autherley Junction might at times doubt this.

Innocent or not, wherever you cruise you meet them, and unless the wind is favourable they stay with you for quite a while. Often they lurk discreetly behind tall hedges like that one between Nuneaton and Atherstone, but the newly built works at the Sawley end of the Trent & Mersey is no shrinking lily.

I haven't counted those I know, but I have a distinct feeling that few cruising days end without at least one encounter with a collection of those circular beds with ever-revolving arms.

SHAFTS

Just as ropes are called straps on canals, so boathooks are called shafts. Well, perhaps they're not the same as boathooks, since they're much bigger, and not usually used for hooking. They are the long sturdy round poles, often striped like barbers' signs, which lie ready to hand on top of any self-respecting canal boat.

A flimsy river-going boathook would be useless anyhow, for normally your shaft has a tough job to do, pushing you off the mud of some shallow canal channel. That is its main job, and no lightweight 6-ft broomhandle could tackle it. Though shafts often have a hook at the end, I've only seen this used for pulling down the top beams of Llangollen, Caldon and Brecon lift-bridges.

Shafts, then, are for shoving—rather like the Broads quant but for different reasons. So respect your shaft, and never ever put it on the ground. You're sure to forget it, and even more certain to need it in the next mile or so.

SHOPPING

There are two ways of solving the problem of supplies for a canal cruise. You either take vast quantities with you—including those absurd triangular packets of everlasting milk—or you live off the land as you go along. The latter is far more fascinating if a little precarious; for even in these days of national and international production of standardised foods, it is surprising how often the shops on your journey will sell things that you have never seen or heard of before.

This applies not only to local delicacies such as the black puddings near bridge 59B above Wigan, or the mysterious contents of butchers' shops in Thorne, but also to such common things as tinned grapefruit, sausages, sauce, cornflakes, pickled onions, and especially fizzy minerals. These last cause you to end up with a museum-worthy collection of different firms' bottles that nobody will give you any money for.

Stronger drink, too, still varies remarkably in between the great brewery chains, and you'll even meet pubs like one on the Gloucester-Sharpness Canal that sells local-brewed cider. Milk tastes much more refreshing if you've had to chase a cart seen disappearing down a nearby street—one of the most energetic of canal-cruising activities. Vegetables, of course, are much more likely to be real if they are bought from a canal-side cottage.

Buying in new places, then, fills your table with a wealth of unknown names, and possibly even with unknown tastes. Try, for example, the butcher just before the crossroads at Stourport, another at Great Haywood, another by bridge 65 at Lapworth, and have a go at the Noble Pies of Newark.

The national chains of supermarkets differ little, but it is the small shops that are the ones to go for, and which perhaps deserve some support in these throat-cutting days. In particular I would put in a plea for shopping in village shops—for there are always villages just up the road from many of the lonely bridges. There you can actually talk about what you buy to someone who knows about it—and who will as like as not cut you a lettuce straight from his own back garden.

SHORT BOATS

The infuriating aspect of the Leeds & Liverpool Canal for the owners of full-length narrow boats is that they can't cruise along it, although its locks are 14 ft wide. Between Leeds and

Wigan those locks—eighty-five of them—are only 62 ft long (which, however, is still longer than the Calder & Hebble's at 57 ft 6 in). So don't turn up hopefully without measuring your boat first.

Cruising the Leeds & Liverpool with something short enough

still brings you occasional sights of those fascinating barges built to fit these locks and known as short boats. Indeed, until quite recently you still met some carrying coal to Wigan power station, and you see such boats now scattered here and there both on the main line and on the Rufford Branch, usually looking sad and neglected. They all seem to have names of boys or girls, and through the years *John* and *Peter* and *Mary* and *Martha Alice* must have ploughed bluntly along, loaded almost to water level, with their great tillers like cart shafts, and their decoration quite different from that of the narrow boats elsewhere.

Some have been converted, and a famous one named *Arthur* has not only found its way miraculously to southern waterways, but has even penetrated well into France. But on the Leeds & Liverpool now, apart from some well-kept maintenance boats roughly the same shape, you can often cruise from one end to the other without seeing a traditional short boat moving.

SIDE PONDS

At Atherstone and Marsworth, Knowle and Diglis basin, and at a surprising number of other odd places up and down the country, you'll see some sort of pond at the side of a lock. It may be so neglected and overgrown that you can barely recognise it, or it may still be clear and filled with water.

These side ponds were cunning devices to prevent the everlasting running away of many thousands of gallons every time a boat went through a lock. We get so used to using locks that we tend to forget what a vast quantity of water disappears downhill each time we go through; and all this water has to be put into the higher level of the canal somehow to start with. When boats used to stream up and down the canals all day long, then the poor old summit levels could hardly collect enough water to keep feeding down the locks.

Hence side ponds. You'll notice that there is, or was, a paddle leading to them. If this is still working, try using it. If you start with a full lock, open this paddle first, so that half your water runs into the side pond until it and the lock are level. Close the paddle and empty the rest of the water from the lock into the pound beneath, leaving half a lockful parked in the side pond. The next chap along—if he's as clever as you—puts this side pond water into the lock first through its own paddle. Then he closes the paddle and fills the remaining part of the lock from the pound up above. Each time half a lockful of water is saved, simply by shunting it backwards and forwards into this water park at the side.

Unhappily, though you'll see plenty of side ponds about, most of the paddles seem to be broken now, and you may travel a long way before you can have the interesting experience of using one. At Diglis basin you can see the lock-keeper conserving water from the Worcester & Birmingham Canal instead of running it all through his broad locks into the Severn.

SIGNPOSTS

Not many years ago it was possible to lose oneself on canals, especially on such thoughtless stretches as the Bridgewater, where there aren't even names or numbers on the bridges to guide you. Most of the trouble occurred at junctions, for often canals have the habit of not going where you think they ought to go at those points.

At Napton, for example, many a traveller from Braunston must have gone straight on hoping to get to Birmingham, when in fact he should have swung round to the right and tried to avoid adding to the many scars on the bridge there. And how many mystified boaters have ended up in the milk-churn-haunted basin at Ellesmere when they thought they were roaring up to Llangollen?

Fortunately quite a number of signposts have been put up recently, thus preventing some boaters from wandering helplessly about the network for the rest of their lives. The old sign at Napton used to point straight down to the bed of the canal for Birmingham. The latest posts have been rather pleasantly coloured in the style of the old tall signposts now disappearing from our country lanes.

The BCN still seems to be using a stencil for some of its notices, and there's a surprising recent signpost at Horsley Fields that sends you up the Wyrley & Essington by calmly telling you that it leads to Cannock. In fact you haven't been able to get beyond the Sneyd hairpin or the A5 at Norton Canes for years. Maybe this was erected by an old canal man I met recently at Tividale, who also insisted that the canal still ran to the collieries near Cannock.

There's room for more signposts yet. The Thames and the Oxford canals, for example, largely ignore each other around their junctions at Oxford. I met a rather worried couple towing a little boat on the Old Main Line near Birmingham who had obviously taken the wrong turn at Factory Junction, and had to brave the chemicals of Oldbury, the legs of the motorway, and the junk of the Smethwick Three, as penalties for missing the three Factory Locks to the broad New Main Line.

There must be quite a few people, too, who overshoot the top lock at Wigan, and set off along what might once have been the rest of the Lancaster Canal, instead of turning right to tackle the mighty 21. Fortunately in this case they can't get far.

SILLS

At the top end of every lock, lurking under the water when the lock is full, is a solid lump of stone or concrete called a sill (or cill), whose job it is to hold the top gates against the weight of the water in the pound above. This really doesn't concern us unless we are in a full-size narrow boat, or in a smaller boat occupying the back of the lock as the water drops.

If we are in fact sitting too close to these top gates when the lock empties, the boat may well descend on to this sill, with its propeller and rudder, which won't do either any good. Indeed, it is possible to break the back of a longish boat if it settles down like this.

The moral, therefore, is to keep away from these gates, or at least to make sure how far the sill extends into the lock. Some sills project further than others, and now and again some good fairy has painted a mark on the lock side to indicate where the sill is going to be. Coming uphill in locks, of course, you can often see the whole thing exposed before you begin to fill the lock, and massive sights some sills look.

Commercial boatmen sometimes used to save time and money by using a lock sill as an unofficial drydock, sitting their sterns on the sill and gently lowering the water until they could get at the propeller and rudder. Needless to say this was quite improper, and certainly likely to be unpopular with any other boat waiting to use the lock.

SLURPS

This word was invented by a young crew member of mine some years ago. Every so often along canals you see a sort of overflow lip slightly above water level, obviously to release water if for any reason the level gets too high. As you pass these things your boat first of all sucks the water away from them, and then slops some of it over the lip in little waves. My crewman felt that 'slurp' was as good a name as any, so slurps they have become, and I have never discovered their official name.

Some of the slurps on the Shropshire Union, especially on those great embankments, are rather alarming in their steepness, and there's a fine specimen just south of Norbury. Slurps elsewhere seem instead to trickle gently into the nearest ditch, but they come in all sorts of shapes and sizes, occasionally accompanied by lost-looking paddle-gear to control a sluice somewhere.

I've never found out where the water eventually goes to if it ever does run over a slurp in any quantity. But now and again we make up interesting stories about a slurp-world in the bowels of the earth, containing every little wave and overflow that ever crossed the hundreds of slurp-lips throughout the canal system.

SPLIT BRIDGES

On some canals you come across a rather alarming sight, at least from the boat—a bridge with a gap in the middle, the two halves seemingly suspended in the air. These bridges are in fact quite safe, having hung there for a considerable time (indeed, some of them have sagged a little and closed the gap, thus being even safer).

The idea is, of course, to save money, since by making a gap in the middle the builders didn't have to construct the bridge wide enough to run a towpath underneath. Instead, the horse went round and the rope went through the gap. Most of these bridges are footbridges at locks—some narrow, some wide—but on the Stratford Canal several farm bridges have splits in them.

Those canallers who prefer to tow their boats in and out of locks are grateful for these slits of old, especially in Heartbreak Hill.

See also FIELD BRIDGES and FOOTBRIDGES.

STAIRCASES

Sometimes, as on most of the Oxford, for example, locks are gently scattered along the route. Elsewhere, where the canal builders met hills or watersheds, they are gathered more closely together in 'flights' (see WIGAN, HATTON and TARDE-BIGGE). But here and there, where the slope is even sharper, you meet a 'staircase', or 'riser', and this means that you move from one lock straight into the next without a pound in between.

Bingley (see p 21) is usually spoken of with awe as the king of staircases, but in fact on the Caledonian Canal there's a staircase of eight locks in a pile compared with Bingley's mere five. Few of us get our boats up there, however, but it's as well to bear Banavie in mind when boasting of Bingley.

There are several little staircases on the canals in England, too, which are often forgotten by the guides. Two locks adjoining at Bascote on the Grand Union used to catch numerous surprised travellers, who ended up by flooding the bottom lock sides when they let water out of the top, till a notice was put up at the side. There are two staircase-pairs within the basin at Stourport that are hardly ever mentioned, and another pair starts you off on your way up the interesting Caldon. Right in the middle of the BCN the easily worked staircase at Brades helps you on your way from the Old Line to the New on the Gower Branch. A pair of locks in the Stourbridge flight almost qualify as a staircase, but in fact have a yard or two between them and thus match themselves with Bratch instead (see p 31).

Other staircases are better known. Bunbury pair on the Shroppie are perhaps more familiar than the less-visited and slow-filling three at Chester further along. Everyone knows of Grindley Brook on the Llangollen, and also of Foxton and Watford on the Leicester, which I mention elsewhere. What people often forget, however, is that in addition to the Five-Rise at Bingley on the Leeds & Liverpool, there are no less than seven other staircases on that canal, all of them at the Yorkshire end. Three contain two locks, and four contain three locks.

Despite airy statements in some guides, the same lock-working rules don't apply to all staircases. In theory, if a lower lock is full, you can't empty an upper lock into it, since it will overflow; but in fact there are safeguards against this in some staircases, though not in others. At Bunbury I've seen torrents of water over the bottom gate sweep boats back through the bridge, as someone emptied a full top lock into a full bottom one. But the upper pair in Stourport basin, the pair at the Caldon entrance, and the Botterham pair on the Staffs & Worcs, for example, each have a lip at the side of the lower lock below the lock edge. Thus water running into an already full lock merely overflows this safety lip. Some of the Leeds & Liverpool staircases appear to have a safety exit, too, taking surplus water into the weir that is passing the staircase. Of course, Foxton and Watford work on a different principle by having elongated side ponds to take care of surplus water.

All the same, it's a safe principle to ensure that before you empty one lock into a lower one, the one below is already at its low level. In this way you can use one lockful of water to take you down from lock to lock till you emerge at the bottom. Or, conversely, when you start up with your empty lock at the bottom, make sure you have full ones above you that can empty in turn into the succeeding vacancies in the locks below.

It's all very confusing, however, especially if you read those complicated instructions in the official guides, which seem to have you running up and down, half opening this paddle and that, until you don't know where you are, and probably end up draining the locks completely. Luckily, there often seems to be some official or unofficial chap there to direct operations, so you thankfully leave it to him.

One aspect of narrow-lock staircases is awkward at busy times: once a boat has started ascending or descending, boats at the other end must wait until he's through. If they don't happen to realise this and set out, the classic irresistible force meets the classic immovable object. Fortunately this doesn't apply with narrow canal boats meeting each other in broad staircases, such as Bingley, Bunbury and Bascote. There you can have the weird experience of passing another boat in the same lock, while you go one way and he goes the other. Most people don't believe this is possible, but try it in a broad staircase sometime.

STANDEDGE

This tunnel on the unfortunately closed Huddersfield Narrow Canal is famous for two reasons: (1) it's the longest canal tunnel in Britain, and (2) its length seems to vary alarmingly according to where you happen to read about it. At various times I have read of lengths of 5,415 yd, 5,456 yd, 5,595 yd, and 5,716 yd (the last but one, I believe, because a printer somewhere slipped up between 3 miles 135 yd and 3 miles 315 yd).

I am indebted to Charles Hadfield and Gordon Biddle for what seems to be the truth of the matter. The tunnel was originally 3 miles 176 yd long, but had 32 yd removed when a railway was built across the end at an angle. In place of the 32 yd an extension was built up with girders and floor plates for 274 yd. Thus if you would care to check the whole tunnel with a tape measure it should be 3 miles 418 yd long, or 5,698 yd.

It is sad that this canal is closed, but apparently navigating the tunnel was a hair-raising experience. I believe that occasionally permission is given for small boats to explore it still, though it now has locked gates across each end. Although it is little more than 7 ft wide now, with a number of passing places, it cost a lot of time and money to build. It was opened in 1811 before a crowd of 10,000 and with a band playing, the first boat taking 1 hour and 40 minutes to go through.

Don't be misled by the date 1893 at the Diggle end; that was the year in which they added the extra section that has mixed everybody up ever since.

STEPS

Anyone slogging up Tardebigge is grateful for the solid steps provided in the lock shoulders at the bottom of each lock. Here you can drop a crew member to prepare the lock when going uphill, or pick him up when coming down. Elsewhere on many

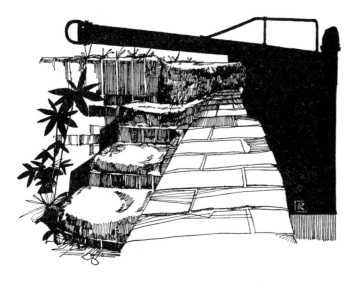

canals such steps are provided in some fashion or other for the lock-worker to move from one level to another.

At deep locks such as Somerton there are steep mounds of worn steps. At many Grand Union broad locks the steps curve round gracefully to avoid the balance beams (though one Warwickshire lock gives up and provides a metal ladder instead). Where there are road bridges, the steps may be claustrophobic and head-cracking, and one set on the Staffs & Worcs is more like a winding stairway to a church belfry.

As with everything else, then, there are all kinds, from the magnificent baronial steps at Northgate in Chester to the crumbling grass-covered ones on rural canals. Often there are none, and you descend or ascend an ancient grassy slope.

STOKE BRUERNE

This is the one canal name known to many people, since they turn up in thousands every year to see the remarkable canal museum by the waterside. The village has always been canal-orientated, since it is strategically placed where the waterway has just climbed seven locks and is about to plunge into

Blisworth's mighty hole. Canal people have always lived there, and canal enthusiasts have now joined or replaced them. There's a pub opposite attractive cottages, and boats always around, though the regular chug of the Grand Union's coal run has almost faded away.

The lovingly tended museum must have converted many an adult and many a youngster into canal addicts. It preserves large numbers of articles, pictures and records of the past that might have been lost for ever.

STOPPAGE

This is an ominously descriptive word applied to the closing of a section of canal. Usually it is to enable maintenance jobs, especially at locks, to be carried out. Official notices have to be issued announcing the closure of the route for the time needed to do the work.

Unlike similar occurrences on roads, of course, it isn't possible merely to direct traffic round a few side canals until it comes back to the main route again. What alternative route there may be could well take an extra week or so. Indeed, when the Bridgewater announced its own stoppage by bursting its banks in 1971, there was no non-tidal alternative route at all for boats between the northern canals and the rest.

Stoppages can therefore be extremely inconvenient for people using the canals, so on the whole they are imposed outside the busiest cruising times. Two unhappy trends recently, however, have worried boaters who don't just stick to the midsummer months. Firstly, stoppages have been imposed at quite short notice, even during summer, and often for reasons not really connected with the canal at all. A rash of sewers and pipelines have interrupted canal routes as they were laid, though elsewhere pipeline-layers have managed to get under the canal by blocking off half of it at a time and thus leaving a passage. The second trend is even more annoying. This is the growing practice of closing canals for excessively long periods during the winter months in order to get jobs done, with the implication that

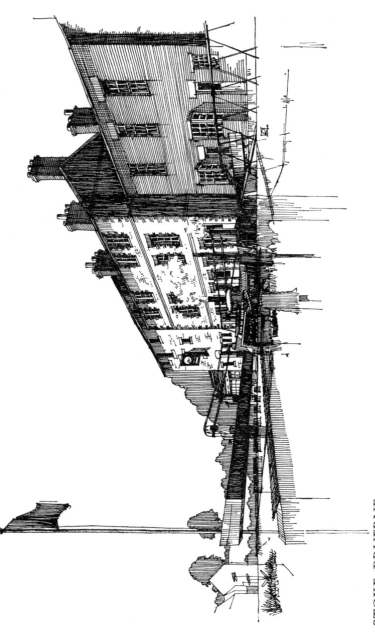

STOKE BRUERNE

nobody should cruise at that time anyhow. The Leicester line has suffered badly from this, with stoppages of many weeks at a time for the rebuilding of locks, sewer-laying, and in one place the replacement of a simple bridge.

When canals were widely used commercially, there would certainly never be stoppages of this length of time even for this sort of job, and more serious canal users are becoming increasingly angry at such happenings. While licences continue to be issued for the whole year, boaters should be able to use the waterways for this period, subject only to necessary stoppages. Moreover, it is bad for waterways such as the Leicester to be completely abandoned by boats for weeks at a time.

Most stoppages, however, are obviously planned to cause the least possible inconvenience, though, in the winter months especially, you have to be on your toes. It once took me 3 months, on and off, to get from Braunston to Shardlow because of a mixture of unpublicised stoppages and frost. Another time I had to abandon the idea of coming down the Leicester, though no notification about a closed lock had reached many officials. No one who has ever had to leave a boat in an unexpected place can imagine the complications of sorting out transport and bedding, and being forced to return home, the voyage half done.

Official planned stoppages are listed and sent out at the beginning of the year, but it's the emergency stoppages and those planned during the year that you have to watch out for. You find notices of these pinned up in all sorts of places, some of them obscure, along the canal system. So keep your eyes skinned for such noticeboards if you don't want to end up in the middle of nowhere, with a lock rebuilding ahead of you and a bridge being demolished behind.

STOP PLANKS

In mysterious neat piles by bridges and locks, or tucked in cubbyholes in bridge abutments, you often see sturdy timber beams. When a lock or a length of canal has to be drained, these planks slide down stop-grooves, one after the other, to form a

dam. You can see the grooves in the stonework of the canal sides nearby, and, of course, locks and narrow bridge-holes are the logical places to put them. Sometimes, instead of planks and grooves, you will see stopgates to swing across the canal, though many of these have rotted now.

Stop planks are also used in emergencies if there is a leak or burst. A striking example of this was the Bridgewater burst in 1971, when quick action confined the drained length to 3 miles instead of nearly 50.

The planks on narrow canals are about 7 ft long, but of course on broad canals they must be at least 14 ft. This makes them very heavy, and often on the Bridgewater you will see a crane by a pile of planks.

STOURPORT

Here's an interesting example of a town that simply wouldn't be there but for the canals, but which virtually turns its back on its canal now. Although it has some magnificent basins full of boats, it is nowadays really a vast road funnel for traffic from the

8

Midlands pouring over the Severn bridge towards Wales. Yet within a stone's throw of them all is this quaint collection of water levels and locks linking the Staffs & Worcs Canal with the river.

All this might not have existed if the canal had gone to Bewdley instead, for that town was already a prosperous trading centre on the Severn. But Brindley went to Lower Mytton, which then became Stourport. A small alehouse became an important waterway town.

Now, if you can find a mooring, it's as pleasant a calling place as you can meet anywhere. You sit there in a little boating world and let the endless road traffic go by almost unheard. There's an awkward deep lock out into the canal, and a curious dog-leg pair of staircases out into the river. Apart from numerous people fishing by the 'No Fishing' notices the basins are utterly relaxing.

STRATFORD-UPON-AVON

Stratford, leaving aside Shakespeare, is well known in waterway circles for two things. First, it has been the hub of two of the most exciting restoration projects in waterway history, but, secondly, the apathy and even downright antagonism of some of its inhabitants to those very projects has disgusted many canal enthusiasts.

The less said about the latter the better, and perhaps Stratford people will learn to be proud of the quieter pleasures offered by their waterways, in contrast to the building of monster (and monstrous) hotels, the clanging of the tills, and the whole rather revolting Shakespeare honky-tonk. But whatever happens, the restoration of the waterways leading to Stratford has become a remarkable piece of history.

The ball was set rolling by the reopening in 1962 of the Lower Avon from Tewkesbury to Evesham—a project inspired and led by Douglas Barwell, whose name will be revered. Later came the Stratford Canal revival, which brought the thirty-six locks of the southern canal back from ruin, and in 1964 boats were once more coming down and emerging in front of the Memorial Theatre to pass through the lock into the river. Now the upper Avon has come through to complete the link, restored with almost indescribable ingenuity, persuasion, and sheer downright doggedness by the same remarkable man, David Hutchings. So Stratford is now a waterway name to take its place with Braunston, Hawkesbury, Fradley, Wigan, Hurleston, and many more in the gallery of cruising landmarks.

SUMMIT LEVELS

Every canal has its highest point. Some, like the Brecon, the Llangollen and the Macclesfield, start at these highest points and step down all the way. Others, such as the Grand Union, rise more than once to high levels before falling again. These 'peaks' on canals are their 'summit levels', and when the canals were built they probably caused the builders more headaches than any other aspect of the work.

The reason is, of course, that every boat using the locks below the summit takes some of the water away from the top—and thus the engineers had to make sure there was a water supply there. The water supply of canals that crossed watersheds, as distinct from those, like the Llangollen, which were fed by a river at their top end, required considerable thought. Not only did the engineers have to supply water to the summit, but they also had to decide when it was wise to give up building locks and drive a tunnel instead.

This last decision would have presented an interesting problem —working out the cost of tunnelling versus building more locks, and calculating the extra journey time locks would impose on boats. But over-riding all this was the supply of the water.

Sometimes, then, as at Tring in the Chilterns, canals climbed all the way over without a tunnel, and the engineers built reservoirs. But at other times the reservoirs were lower and tunnels were dug, as at Blisworth and Braunston further along. One of the possible bonuses of tunnelling was that there might be springs in the ground that would top up the water. The builders of the Basingstoke Canal took a definite gamble on finding springs in the chalk in Greywell tunnel, and it paid off.

Normally, however, high summit levels on canals had to have reservoirs nearby to keep them supplied with water, and all over the system you find such reservoirs. You can see one alongside the Grand Union at Calcutt, and there are several near the Oxford (explore the rushes at Wormleighton); then there are the Foulridge reservoirs near the summit tunnel of the Leeds & Liverpool, and many others if you search around. The intakes from them are sometimes barely visible, but others flow in under striking little bridges, such as the one above Claydon on the Oxford.

One other way in which summit levels were maintained in some places, particularly in the Black Country, was by pumping, even out of old mine-shafts, and there are still pumps at work. The Kennet & Avon is topped up from a reservoir below its summit by means of pumping up to a leat which then runs to the summit. An electric pump replaced the old steam pumps some time ago, but enthusiasts have restored the beam engines at Crofton, and they are brought 'into steam' at certain times during the year. There are also flights of locks—as at Tinsley near Sheffield—where water is regularly pumped back to replace that brought down.

Summit levels are sometimes long and often give us spectacular views where the land falls away on one side or the other. But we still can't take it for granted that they'll stay full of water, and more than once in recent years canals have had to be closed during dry spells. Careless locking, too, can drain water away from a summit.

SWING-BRIDGES see MOVING BRIDGES

TAPS

Human beings, in the Western World anyhow, are so used to an abundant supply of water from a tap that they go along happily using vast quantities when afloat in a canal boat. Inevitably the water-tanks then dry up, often on the first day of a cruise.

Fortunately there are taps at frequent intervals to replenish the boat's supply, but unfortunately transferring the water to the boat isn't always easy.

Often, for example, the tap is alongside a lock, and as soon as you connect up a hosepipe, a queue of boats immediately appears (thank goodness they've now moved the one at Autherley lock!). Or, despite large notices, there are so many unoccupied boats moored in front of the tap that you can't get near it (as at Office Lock, Leeds). Or the tap runs so slowly that you give up in despair (Glascote). Or, most common of all, your hosepipe flies off as soon as you turn the tap on.

Then there are hooligans who have wrecked the tap you were pinning your hopes on, or your hosepipe isn't long enough, or it has a kink in it. So despite the frequency of canal-side taps it is wise to carry a portable water container, which at least you can take to the nearest pub.

TARDEBIGGE

This unusual name lies in canallers' minds along with Wigan, Hatton, and soon perhaps Devizes, to remind them of strenuous climbs up or down lock after lock—twenty-one at Wigan, twenty-one at Hatton, one day maybe even twenty-nine at Devizes, and, according to all the books, a record thirty at Tardebigge.

It's not quite as straightforward as that, however. Wigan and Hatton are broad locks, and thus heavier going, with Wigan's tough gates winning the prize; and to talk of 'thirty locks' at Tardebigge is to mislead, as many a traveller from Birmingham to Worcester has discovered. As you clock up your thirty going downhill you can save your sigh of relief, for round the corner you find another six locks lurking, with no more space between than there was between some of the first thirty. Though you then get a mile or so to breathe through Stoke salt works, six more locks turn up before you get any real rest at all.

So next time you hear of 'the Tardebigge Thirty', remind the

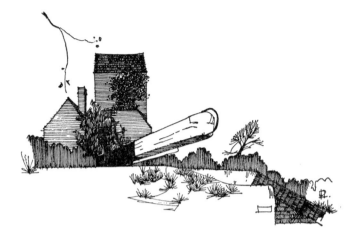

speaker that it's in fact forty-two he's talking about, whatever name they go by.

Tardebigge also not only holds the record for the number of locks in a row but has the deepest narrow canal lock in the country at the top. This, sitting below the slim spire of the church, lowers you 14 ft, and when the Worcester & Birmingham company first faced the long slope to the Severn they actually built an experimental lift just here. There is a fascinating picture of it in Charles Hadfield's *The Canals of the West Midlands*, showing a huge tank suspended from eight great wheels, ready to be raised by two men at windlasses. This lift passed no less than 110 boats in 12 hours one day, but despite this the company decided against using lifts, and went ahead and built locks all the way down—fifty-eight of them before you get into the Severn.

Tardebigge is undoubtedly hard work, but you get into the swing of it. You're intrigued by the solid wood of the gates, the metal rope-hooks set in the lock corners, the weirs which bubble out and throw your steering awry, the steep steps so useful for landing and picking up crew, and the large numbers carved on the lock shoulders—in Arabic numerals rather than the superior Roman of Wigan.

When you've climbed down the thirty, there is, luckily, a

pleasant pub now to refresh you before starting on the next twelve. On a hot summer's day you need it.

TIDES

This may seem another odd topic for canallers, but in fact if you cruise very far, you are sure to come across the effects of tides. You feel this influence most strongly if you're heading for the Chesterfield Canal or the Stainforth & Keaby, for you must use the tidal Trent (see EAGRE). The tidal Thames, too, may concern you if you do the round trip of the Grand Union and Oxford Canals, for you can't just come happily down river and expect to get into Brentford lock at any old time. Even the Severn tide may affect you a little, for at times it comes up to Tewkesbury and even beyond—though here you're not in a tidal estuary.

Adventurous canallers set out sooner or later for the Great Ouse via the Middle Level, and if they manage to get through the weed and the locks, find themselves at Salters Lode waiting for the tidal Ouse to make a level. When it does, you have to nip out smartly before the gates have to be closed again, and you then tootle around a tidal corner and smartly through Denver Sluice before reaching non-tidal waters again.

There are other tidal adventures for boaters, such as the Yorkshire Ouse, the Severn estuary, or even the Wash, but such trips require careful consideration of your boat and the weather, and the services of a pilot.

TILLERS

The true canal steerer steers with a tiller, leaning happily on it or tucking himself just inside the cabin in cold or wet weather. He can't very easily sit down to the job, so his legs sometimes get weary. But there seems to be no getting away from the fact that a tiller is the thing for canals, preferably with a beautiful Turk's Head knot or a horse's tail. You can see one on the narrow boat on p 96.

Most of us mortals, however, for one reason or another, steer with a wheel, usually because the boat has no separate rudder but an outboard motor or an outdrive. The whole driving contraption, including the propeller, turns as we steer. Boatbuilders seem to prefer this system, with a complicated ramification of linkage from the wheel through an enclosed cable to various links on the transom, in order to move the outboard or outdrive. The whole arrangement has a lot of bits and pieces to go wrong, and the works are extremely difficult to get at when it does.

I've seen ingenious handymen attach a tiller to an outboard motor, and I can't see why this shouldn't be done to an outdrive, too. It's not only simpler to get at, but it's much less work to use. It would take a better man than me, however, to devise it.

Meanwhile canal steerers are sharply divided among the experts haughtily standing at their tillers and the vast majority twiddling away at wheels—though the latter can at least thankfully sit down to it.

TOM PUDDINGS see COMPARTMENT BOATS

TOWPATHS

Purists call them towing paths, and of course they are the tracks along the canal side used by horses, mules, donkeys and men to pull boats along. Underneath the thick growth of years, they are still solid brick and stone in many places, as you soon find when you try to knock in a mooring pin. But only too often time or wear, wash or vandals, have pulled the towpaths into the canals; in some places they hardly exist at all, while their big stones lie out in the channel as hazards to boats.

Some canals seem to have had better-built towpaths than others; horsedrawn boats travel stretches of them still and riders and walkers make increasing use of them. Everywhere, of course, anglers sit on them in summer, and sadly some of them leave ample traces of their presence. Towards summer's end the less used towpaths grow a 6-ft fringe of willowherb along the water's edge, with occasional gaps hacked by fishermen. If you ever have to tow a boat on such a towpath, you'll do it with the greatest difficulty.

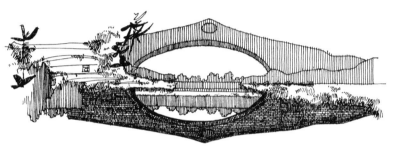

Horses needed a change (or landowners were cantankerous) so now and again a towpath changes sides on a roving or turnover bridge. These were cunningly designed so that the horse could climb up, cross over, come down towards the boat, and continue under the bridge on the other side, without needing to be unfastened from the boat. (You can work this out in the drawing on p 141.) The meaner canal companies presumably wouldn't spend money on such wide bridges, so at both turnover and ordinary bridges they often made the horse go round the bridge while his rope was taken through a slit.

Some of the turnover bridges have delightful shapes, as do many towpath bridges over side-arms or junctions, especially in the BCN and on the Oxford Canal. The Macclesfield, too, has some beauties.

9

TRAFFIC LIGHTS

They do exist along some waterways, though there are hardly queues of boats champing to be off on the amber. As far as I remember there isn't any amber anyway, but on canals such as the Aire & Calder and the Gloucester–Sharpness, and on rivers such as the Trent, Severn and Weaver, there are red and green signals at locks and in some cases at swing-bridges.

Disconcertingly, the chaps with their fingers on the switches don't always bother using the lights for pleasure boats, and if the gates or bridges are open, and you hang about waiting for the light, you often get an abrupt hand signal to proceed. To be honest it does seem a bit absurd, when you can clearly see an empty lock, to have to worry about a green light before you go in. I suppose there are circumstances in which you might be doing the wrong thing, and in some places, anyhow, your view is obstructed. Tewkesbury lock on the Severn, for example, has a fairly blind bend whichever way you approach it, and from the south you can't even see the light till you're almost on top of the gates.

There are one or two bridges also on the Gloucester–Sharpness Ship Canal so placed that you might well come round a corner and find an enormous coaster in your path. The Weaver, too, produces coasters, though here they have their own large lock beside the one you would be using.

The Aire & Calder lights are high above the centre of the lock, and just to make sure of you there are often three reds or greens showing—except where bulbs have failed. My favourite traffic light is at Diglis on the Severn. There you not only get a green but also a little yellow arrow to direct you to the smaller of the two locks. Lower down, where you leave the Severn for Gloucester Docks, the lock not only has traffic lights for you but also a bell that rings to warn anyone crossing the footbridge that the lock gates are about to open.

The keepers of these lights, locks and bridges are an eagle-eyed race. You may think that they are unaware of your approach, but you would nearly always be wrong. The Tewkesbury man has cut himself a gap in the trees so that he can see you a mile away to the south. Their secret is not a sixth sense but the telephone —they ring up and tell each other that you're coming.

TUNNELS

The surprising thing is that every canal tunnel seems to have its individual character—yet they're all just holes through hills.

At the bigger ones in particular I always think with awe about the digging of them. Men with the simplest tools and lights clawed their way through, and in most cases lined the sides with brick or stone and burrowed ventilating shafts. I not only admire the sheer physical effort, but also the fact that they managed to get the things straight—or more or less straight. How, in those days, did they ever manage to meet in the middle after starting from both ends? But meet they did, give or take a few wiggles.

The wiggles have been made worse by subsidence in Barnton and Saltersford, those early tunnels on the northern Trent and Mersey. Indeed, it's difficult to be sure whether there's a boat already in them or not, since the bulges leave only a slit of the far end visible. But it's no good going in until you're certain the tunnel is clear, since you couldn't pass another boat if you met one in either of these two, nor in the straighter Preston Brook further on. At one time the tugs in these tunnels had wheels on their sides to roll along the tunnel walls.

The Llangollen's tunnels are even narrower, and like the aqueducts will only just take your boat. Labouring west through the Chirk tunnel against the unusual flow of this canal can be harassing if your boat has a deep draught.

It really is intriguing to compare tunnels with each other. Little Drakeholes on the Chesterfield has part of its walls looking like worn gargoyles in the soft rock. Some of the southern tunnels of the Worcester & Birmingham have uneven rocky sides which can reach out and bite you. Narrow Curdworth, on the Birmingham & Fazeley, is pretty tricky at the Birmingham end, and in broader Wast Hill on the Worcester & Birmingham you can find yourself in the middle on a misty day without being able to see either end.

The mightier tunnels often have showers of water dropping from the roof here and there, and fascinating multi-coloured ever-wet patterns decorating their sides. There are stalactites, light pouring down shafts, and mysterious side-openings, and I occasionally wonder how often the brickwork is inspected.

The latest and widest tunnel is Netherton (see p 98) on the BCN, and I find this disconcerting to steer through. Normally it is helpful to put on cabin lights as well as your headlamp, so as to see the walls going by. But Netherton, unlike most tunnels, has not one but two towpaths to fend you off. Somehow these, with their protective railings, are more awkward than bare tunnel sides to steer by.

Some people hate canal tunnels, and it's easy to see why when you are deep in the bowels of the earth, with only your own light and power to sustain you. Even the most blasé steerer must feel his adrenalin going round as he approaches another headlamp without knowing what lurks behind it. It may be a small cruiser or a pair of narrow boats, and whichever it is, you know that there's only a few inches to spare in the passing—always provided you've chosen a 14-ft tunnel to start with. When you've thankfully negotiated the job, you find you still haven't the least idea who or what you have passed.

Boats that pass in tunnels are far more mysterious than ships that pass in the night.

See also ARMITAGE, BLISWORTH, HARECASTLE, NETHERTON and STANDEDGE.

TURF LOCKS

Most locks, of course, are box-shaped with vertical sides. There are diamond-shaped ones on the Warwickshire Avon, and two others on the Oxford Canal where the Cherwell has flowed in and out of it. But if you find yourself on the Kennet & Avon, there are still a few of the original turf-lined sloping-sided locks to go through.

When the Kennet was made navigable in 1723, there were twenty locks between Reading and Newbury, and most of them were built in this economical way. At its lower level the water lay between timber walls about 2 ft above the water level, but the lock sides above these sloped at about 45 degrees outwards, and were covered with turf. This was obviously a cheap way of building locks, and though they held much more water than normal locks, this didn't matter in a river navigation.

When going downstream through these locks, of course, boats had to be careful not to find themselves sitting on the slope. Nowadays there are guard rails to keep you in the middle.

TURK'S HEAD see TILLERS

TURNOVER BRIDGES see TOWPATHS

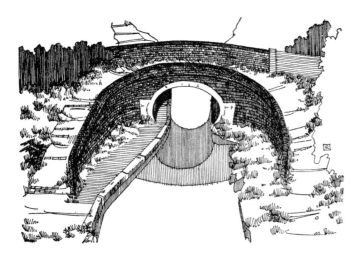

WARDLE CANAL

No guidebook is published to help you along this waterway, and no lists of distances, locks, pubs, bridges and shopping facilities either. Yet if you take the unexpected turn from the Trent & Mersey at Middlewich towards the Shropshire Union, you have to cruise the Wardle Canal.

If you're in doubt about this, look closely at the junction bridge just below Kings Lock. 'Wardle Canal, 1827', says a carved stone; and for 100 yd, including a lock, you cruise this sawn-off waterway. As soon as the top of the lock closes behind you, however, you're in the Shropshire Union.

This ridiculous fact is just another reminder of the cantankerous Trent & Mersey company, which fought off other companies and competition tooth and nail. Even when it allowed them to approach it, it insisted on owning the last bit of water itself, and charging heavy tolls. It did this with the Macclesfield, owning the first $1\frac{1}{2}$ miles to the Hall Green stop lock, where it even refused the passage of boats if its own water happened to be any higher at the time.

So don't forget to enter the Wardle in your logbook. While its solitary lock is filling or emptying, you'll have ample time to explore the whole canal, inch by inch.

WASH

I'm not referring to that activity sometimes avoided by canallers (see BEARDS), but to the movement of water behind a boat. Innocent as this movement may look, too much of it has in fact done more harm than anything else to canal channels. Since motors were fitted in boats, the wash of those boats along banks and towpaths has slowly pulled in mud and even bricks and large stones. That's why you can never find a mooring along some stretches.

Commercial boats were not such culprits as the more recent overpowered and wrongly shaped light cruisers better suited to rivers and the sea. It isn't always a question of speed. Quite small boats moving slowly can often put out big waves, slopping people's tea into their saucers and skidding frying pans off gas rings, as well as filling up the canal bed.

What a lot of boaters don't seem to realise is that you can sometimes roar your engine till it deafens you without producing a scrap of extra speed. All you produce is a breaking wave along either bank and curses from every moored boat that you pass.

Technical boffins assure us that whatever you do it's almost impossible to move at much more than 3 or $3\frac{1}{2}$ mph on a canal, however much speed a roaring engine *sounds* to be doing. You can do this speed with your engine just ticking over and hardly a ripple following you.

So what on earth is the point of using up fuel in large quantities, slowly ruining the canals, and yet not getting anywhere? If you really want to kick up a big wash, try the motorway.

WATER VOLES

These lovable little creatures, which some people squeal at and wrongly call rats, lead a harmless sort of existence as they share the canals with us. They always seem to be busy going somewhere, often carrying a bit of reed, but they seem to lose their cool when a boat comes. With an audible plop they vanish under water, but if you can leave your steering long enough to watch, you'll soon see them come up again somewhere else.

Their ears and tails are shorter than those of rats, and in fact they're more like little beavers. They are mostly vegetarians, and put the front doors of their nests below water level, though the chamber itself is, of course, higher up in the bank.

WATFORD GAP

This place always sounds as if it's some vital pass in a range of mountains, but it never seems to me to be more than a few feet lower than the rather insignificant hills around it. All the same, over the years it has gathered the A5, the Leicester Grand Union (which was 'Grand Union' before anyone else thought of it), the railway, and now the M1, all within a stone's throw of each other on their way to penetrate the fastnesses of the north. So now it's quite a bustling area (in Northants) in the middle of nowhere—even if most people do confuse it with another Watford further south (in Herts).

Watford is intriguing to canallers for two reasons. Firstly, you can now tie up, climb over a fence, and have a tuck-in at a motorway service station—which is historically amusing; and secondly, you have an interesting flight of seven locks, four of which are in staircase form with long side ponds for their water. These locks, with those at Foxton 21 miles further on, helped to make a notorious bottleneck which ever since has prevented boats wider than 7 ft from navigating from the south of England to the north, or vice versa.

If you ever find yourself going north at Watford one day, make sure you fill up with fuel at the A5 alongside you, or you might be sorry during the next few hours.

WEED

No canal trip would be complete without weeds and reeds—especially in late summer. Reeds are, on the whole, decorative and grow at the sides, and I have mentioned some of them under FLOWERS; but underwater weed is one of those fascinatingly infuriating mysteries, quite unpredictable in type, habit and location—at least to the layman. To most people it remains one of those unfortunate necessities of canalling, nameless but inevitable.

Along the more popular canals the weed gets pretty well chopped down by the frequent passage of boats, and indeed this is one of the best cures for it. But anybody exploring lesser-used waterways, or wandering too near to the side of some of the popular ones, will soon find his propeller doing a sort of kitchen-mincer trick.

Lurking under the water may be a variety of curious growths whose real names I leave to the experts. At one end of the scale are masses of huge leaves looking for all the world like cabbage leaves. These seem to prefer rivers such as the Nene, but are also found in the fresher canals. Their nuisance value is in their stalks, for the leaves seem to shred fairly easily. The former, however, are often like tough old lengths of rope, twining lovingly round propeller, rudder and the rest, and maybe snapping shear-pins like carrots.

At the other end of the scale are various weeds that kinder souls liken to cotton wool or blankets, but which seem at times more like steel wool or even wire-netting. They grow in great trailing masses, and cleverly ball themselves around your prop until it keeps on turning but no longer drives you along, since its shape has been entirely changed. This can be rather disconcerting until you realise what has happened. If you would care to experiment with it, try the Chesterfield.

A gleaming new propeller ought to be able to cut weeds into mint sauce, but unfortunately few propellers on canals stay like that. They develop bent and ragged edges from more solid obstacles, so that they are rarely capable of chopping up weeds, and you often have to do some chopping yourself. This can be done precariously through a weed-hatch, which is designed so that you can plunge your arm into the water and fumble blindly with the invisible stuff that you have collected. Or it can be done much more conveniently with an outdrive or outboard unit, which enables you to lift the propeller out of the water.

I would heartily recommend, in any case, a strong waterproof glove for the operation. The jagged edges of the propeller may not be able to chop weed, but they can certainly chop humans, even when they are not turning.

WEIRS

Among the several surprises of the Llangollen are the rushing weirs beside the locks, often streaming with great lengths of weed. They come out with such force at some locks that they sabotage the most careful steerer as he tries to enter the locks.

The reason for these extra-powerful weirs on this particular canal is unusual. The Llangollen carries a steady flow of water all the way down from the Dee at Horseshoe Falls to the reservoir that looms over the four entrance locks at Hurleston. We have this water supply, in fact, to thank for having the canal still

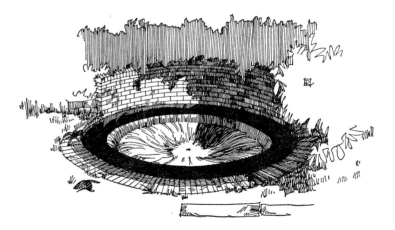

navigable, for it was officially closed for some time. The result is that the canal flows almost like a small river, with a current quite noticeable at times, especially through the tunnels and aqueducts.

There are weirs at most groups of other canal locks, of course, hopefully moving water along and perhaps struggling to keep pounds level against the idiosyncrasies of lock-workers. The designing of these weirs seems to have been one of the fields in which different canal builders let themselves go.

There are those remarkable circular or diamond-shaped disappearing tricks on the Staffs & Worcs, where the water vanishes underground through a large grating (sometimes in somebody's garden), to reappear below the lock. There are narrow rushing open channels on the Northampton flight, broad waterfalls at Hatton, and magnificent foaming torrents at Black Delph when you open the paddle above. Then there are those treacherous little bubbling weirs along Tardebigge, which don't come out a decent distance away from the lock-tail but gurgle right beside you as you enter or leave, so that you wonder what on earth is pushing you up against the side even when there's no wind.

The Leeds & Liverpool has a variety of weirs, as befits its Pennine-crossing magnificence. Some of them come down like mountain streams and, as is to be expected, these attract anglers.

Weirs are mysterious, and I've never entirely fathomed them. The canal authorities keep a close eye on whether they are in fact 'running' or not, for this no doubt indicates whether the vital supply to the highest levels is sufficient. I've seen strange measuring devices at such places as Blackburn and Wigan, which is perhaps a clue as to why the lock-keepers at Wigan are now called Water Controllers.

WHEEL see TILLERS

WIGAN

Wigan Pier exists, even if it's only a mound just round the corner from the canal maintenance yard. But Wigan brands itself on the canaller's mind and muscle not by its pier or its black puddings, but by its twenty-three locks. Two of them are below the junction from Manchester by which most people arrive at the Leeds & Liverpool, leaving a notorious twenty-one to start the climb towards Leeds. They begin quietly, a little spread out, but they go up and up remorselessly, with their big horizontally brooding balance beams stacking up over the town and into the distance.

You are remote from Wigan itself, passing much empty ground as you begin to look down on the houses, but there really isn't much time for sightseeing as you heave at your windlass (or more often, a fixed one), at the wooden arms of the heavy sliding cloughs in the ground at most lock-tops, or at the massive beams themselves. In between you may be tying up to the bollards or shinning up and down ladders if you manage to get your boat near them. Torrents of water pour in from the gate-paddle openings if you've been rash enough to uncover them too soon, instalments of gongoozlers appear seemingly from holes in the ground, you pass under the rare road or railway, and gradually you rise majestically over a panorama dominated by the town below.

At last you approach the top, where—if I've counted them correctly—there are no less than three pubs nearby. There, at right-angles to you, you join 10 miles of the one-time Lancaster Canal, which never had the pleasure of joining its main line, and was thus sunk without trace into the Leeds & Liverpool. Don't forget to turn left and not right.

Canallers talk proudly of Tardebigge and Hatton, but until they've been up Wigan they haven't really lived.

WINDING-HOLES

Every now and again along a canal you come across a curious bulge in the waterway, eating into the field opposite the towpath. Sometimes these places are clear and deep, sometimes they're obscured by reeds and rushes. They are, of course, turning places for full-length narrow boats.

The name 'winding-hole' is pronounced like the wind that blows and not like the wind that raises paddles. Whether this is because boatmen used to use the wind in helping them to turn I've never discovered, but I've certainly used it myself on gusty days.

Some of these winding-holes are in mysterious places in the middle of nowhere, and it's puzzling now why any boat should have wanted to turn round just there. There's one on the Worcester & Birmingham where a trip boat turns round and then proceeds backwards for part of its journey—an alarming sight in the dark—and you have to do the same thing down the Welford Arm if you wish to moor at the end.

If you have to use a winding-hole, it's as well to make sure that it is still in operation. Only too often the vital part is only a few inches deep, and you find yourself jammed sideways across the channel.

WINDLASSES

You're stuck if you lose your windlass, except at places on the Leeds & Liverpool, or the Nene, and at other locks here and there where handles are fixed on the gear. Otherwise you can sit there for ever and not be able to get through a lock. Well, that isn't quite true; I have seen some laborious work with mole wrenches and adjustable spanners, but generally speaking you need the dear old cranked handle in order to work locks.

A highly polished windlass, preferably of brass, is a status symbol among boaters, though there is also a certain amount of kudos attached to owning a huge rusty Leeds & Liverpool contraption, which has a longer throw and can hardly be lifted. The simplest versions of either are plain pieces of metal whose handles are gradually polished by the palms of your hands, though the softer ones among us tend to have kinds with revolving handles. These are easier on the palms, but they tend to nip bits from the hand at each end of the revolving part.

Since there are two different sizes of spindle on paddle-gear (or three if you count the rather smaller Trent & Mersey one), it's necessary either to carry two windlasses, with different-sized holes, or to fall in with the more common habit of using a windlass with a pair of holes fixed side by side at its end. This should cope with most of the locks you'll meet, though it isn't much good on the Calder & Hebble, where you must use a handspike.

There are interesting bits of windlass lore. Besides having a polished handle (the polish can be hastened by steel wool and sandpaper) the aficionado wears his windlass in apparently precarious positions—either down the back of his neck or in his belt—and he never puts it down. This last is a useful rule to imitate, since the lock sides of Britain are regularly strewn with forgotten windlasses (which always disappear before you can get back to look for them). If you place them on balance beams they merely vanish into the depths of the lock, where keen frogmen could make small fortunes.

Two other rules about windlasses are worth following. Firstly, never leave one on a spindle after winding up a paddle. Ratchets being what they are, the harmless bit of bent metal can become a rapidly spinning lethal weapon, which if it doesn't break your arm or knock your eye out, will certainly end up in the lock. Secondly, don't tempt fate by carrying only one windlass on the boat. Take a spare—or maybe five.

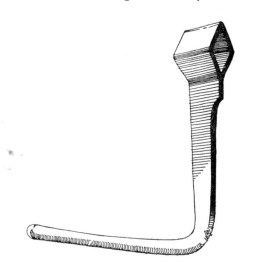